OPPOSING
VIEWPOINTS®
SERIES

The Fifth Estate:
Extreme Viewpoints
from Alternative Media

Other Books of Related Interest

Opposing Viewpoints Series

Internet Censorship
Journalism
Mass Media
Whistleblowers

At Issue Series

Media Bias
What Is the Impact of Cyberlife
When Is Free Speech Hate Speech?
Wikileaks

Current Controversies Series

The Global Impact of Social Media
Media Ethics
Politics and Media

> "Congress shall make no law ... abridging the freedom of speech, or of the press."

First Amendment to the US Constitution

The basic foundation of our democracy is the First Amendment guarantee of freedom of expression. The Opposing Viewpoints series is dedicated to the concept of this basic freedom and the idea that it is more important to practice it than to enshrine it.

OPPOSING
VIEWPOINTS®
SERIES

The Fifth Estate: Extreme Viewpoints from Alternative Media

Kathryn Roberts, Book Editor

GREENHAVEN
PUBLISHING

Published in 2018 by Greenhaven Publishing, LLC
353 3rd Avenue, Suite 255, New York, NY 10010

Articles in Greenhaven Publishing anthologies are often edited for length to meet page
requirements. In addition, original titles of these works are changed to clearly present
the main thesis and to explicitly indicate the author's opinion. Every effort is made to
ensure that Greenhaven Publishing accurately reflects the original intent of the authors.
Every effort has been made to trace the owners of the copyrighted material.

Cover image: ESB Professional/Shutterstock.com

Library of Congress Cataloging-in-Publication Data

Names: Roberts, Kathryn, 1990- editor.
Title: The fifth estate : extreme viewpoints from alternative media / Kathryn
  Roberts, book editor.
Description: First edition. | New York : Greenhaven Publishing, 2018. |
  Series: Opposing viewpoints | Includes bibliographical references and
  index. | Audience: Grades 9-12.
Identifiers: LCCN 2017035962| ISBN 9781534501775 (library bound) | ISBN
  9781534501836 (pbk.)
Subjects: LCSH: Alternative mass media.
Classification: LCC P96.A44 F54 2018 | DDC 302.23--dc23
LC record available at https://lccn.loc.gov/2017035962

Manufactured in the United States of America

Website: http://greenhavenpublishing.com

Contents

Chapter 1: What Potential Does Alternative Media Have to Influence Society?

Chapter 2: How Does Alternative Media Enable Extremist Civil Conflict?

Chapter 3: How Does Technology Help Alternative Media?

Chapter 4: Is It Advantageous to Utilize Alternative Media?

The Importance of Opposing Viewpoints

Perhaps every generation experiences a period in time in which the populace seems especially polarized, starkly divided on the important issues of the day and gravitating toward the far ends of the political spectrum and away from a consensus-facilitating middle ground. The world that today's students are growing up in and that they will soon enter into as active and engaged citizens is deeply fragmented in just this way. Issues relating to terrorism, immigration, women's rights, minority rights, race relations, health care, taxation, wealth and poverty, the environment, policing, military intervention, the proper role of government—in some ways, perennial issues that are freshly and uniquely urgent and vital with each new generation—are currently roiling the world.

If we are to foster a knowledgeable, responsible, active, and engaged citizenry among today's youth, we must provide them with the intellectual, interpretive, and critical-thinking tools and experience necessary to make sense of the world around them and of the all-important debates and arguments that inform it. After all, the outcome of these debates will in large measure determine the future course, prospects, and outcomes of the world and its peoples, particularly its youth. If they are to become successful members of society and productive and informed citizens, students need to learn how to evaluate the strengths and weaknesses of someone else's arguments, how to sift fact from opinion and fallacy, and how to test the relative merits and validity of their own opinions against the known facts and the best possible available information. The landmark series Opposing Viewpoints has been providing students with just such critical-thinking skills and exposure to the debates surrounding society's most urgent contemporary issues for many years, and it continues to serve this essential role with undiminished commitment, care, and rigor.

The key to the series's success in achieving its goal of sharpening students' critical-thinking and analytic skills resides in its title—

Opposing Viewpoints. In every intriguing, compelling, and engaging volume of this series, readers are presented with the widest possible spectrum of distinct viewpoints, expert opinions, and informed argumentation and commentary, supplied by some of today's leading academics, thinkers, analysts, politicians, policy makers, economists, activists, change agents, and advocates. Every opinion and argument anthologized here is presented objectively and accorded respect. There is no editorializing in any introductory text or in the arrangement and order of the pieces. No piece is included as a "straw man," an easy ideological target for cheap point-scoring. As wide and inclusive a range of viewpoints as possible is offered, with no privileging of one particular political ideology or cultural perspective over another. It is left to each individual reader to evaluate the relative merits of each argument—as he or she sees it, and with the use of ever-growing critical-thinking skills—and grapple with his or her own assumptions, beliefs, and perspectives to determine how convincing or successful any given argument is and how the reader's own stance on the issue may be modified or altered in response to it.

This process is facilitated and supported by volume, chapter, and selection introductions that provide readers with the essential context they need to begin engaging with the spotlighted issues, with the debates surrounding them, and with their own perhaps shifting or nascent opinions on them. In addition, guided reading and discussion questions encourage readers to determine the authors' point of view and purpose, interrogate and analyze the various arguments and their rhetoric and structure, evaluate the arguments' strengths and weaknesses, test their claims against available facts and evidence, judge the validity of the reasoning, and bring into clearer, sharper focus the reader's own beliefs and conclusions and how they may differ from or align with those in the collection or those of their classmates.

Research has shown that reading comprehension skills improve dramatically when students are provided with compelling, intriguing, and relevant "discussable" texts. The subject matter of these collections could not be more compelling, intriguing, or urgently relevant to today's students and the world they are poised to inherit. The anthologized articles and the reading and discussion questions that are included with them also provide the basis for stimulating, lively, and passionate classroom debates. Students who are compelled to anticipate objections to their own argument and identify the flaws in those of an opponent read more carefully, think more critically, and steep themselves in relevant context, facts, and information more thoroughly. In short, using discussable text of the kind provided by every single volume in the Opposing Viewpoints series encourages close reading, facilitates reading comprehension, fosters research, strengthens critical thinking, and greatly enlivens and energizes classroom discussion and participation. The entire learning process is deepened, extended, and strengthened.

For all of these reasons, Opposing Viewpoints continues to be exactly the right resource at exactly the right time—when we most need to provide readers with the critical-thinking tools and skills that will not only serve them well in school but also in their careers and their daily lives as decision-making family members, community members, and citizens. This series encourages respectful engagement with and analysis of opposing viewpoints and fosters a resulting increase in the strength and rigor of one's own opinions and stances. As such, it helps make readers "future ready," and that readiness will pay rich dividends for the readers themselves, for the citizenry, for our society, and for the world at large.

Introduction

The Fifth Estate refers to people or groups of people who have what are considered to be outlying viewpoints compared to those that are commonly held in contemporary society. It is an extension of the classical concept called the Estates of the Realm. The Estates of the Realm is a broad social hierarchy used during the medieval and early modern periods of Europe, specifically in France. The clergy represented the First Estate, the nobles represented the Second Estate, and peasants and the bourgeoisie (or broadly, the commoners) represented the Third Estate. Today there is the Fourth Estate, which is not directly linked to the government but contains some of the most significant influence on today's society because it represents what we know to be the traditional news media.

In the United States, the Fourth Estate is used to emphasize the independence of the press, as guaranteed by the US Constitution and the First Amendment, which reads: *Congress shall make no law respecting an establishment of religion, or prohibiting the free exercise thereof; or abridging the freedom of speech, or of the press; or the right of the people peaceably to assemble, and to petition the Government for a redress of grievances.* In this way, the Fourth Estate is used to keep the US government both accountable and transparent.

The Fifth Estate's origins in the United States trace back to the counterculture in the 1960s, in part due to the influence of an underground newspaper, *The Fifth Estate*, which was published in Detroit, Michigan, in 1965. Today, the Fifth Estate is often associated with bloggers and independent journalists who publish via non-mainstream media (with the mainstream media being represented by outlets like ABC, Fox News, CNN, MSNBC, the *New York Times*, etc.). With the advent of the Internet and expansion of digital media, the scope and reach of the Fifth Estate has expanded in a way that allows one of its goals to be to keep the other four estates accountable and unbiased in a way that the mainstream media (specifically the Fourth Estate) is perceived to be.

Conversely, the Fifth Estate is referenced somewhat pejoratively as the "alternative media" because it tends to report in a way that challenges society's dominantly held beliefs and culture. The alternative media places an emphasis on many controversial topics, such as human rights, the environment and climate change, civil rights, and race. Recently, extreme action has been taken by groups such as the "hacktivist" organization Anonymous or Julian Assange's WikiLeaks. These organizations work to bring to light what they believe to be extreme and potentially illegal actions taken by the US government and other governments around the world. These actions also have direct influences on "radical" and "extremist" conflict growing around the world, specifically in the Middle East.

Another aspect of the Fifth Estate and alternative media is that it brings elements of press freedoms to autocratic countries and other places where governments pose extreme restrictions on access to the free press. New technologies like satellite-based radio and television give often-oppressed groups a voice and greater foothold and also allow an easier spread of democracy into these countries. This expanded influence will usher the world into a potentially better-educated society that protects the outspoken from autocratic oppression.

Opposing Viewpoints: The Fifth Estate: Extreme Viewpoints from Alternative Media examines this element's impact on society in chapters titled "What Potential Does Alternative Media Have to Influence Society?," "How Does Alternative Media Enable Extremist Civil Conflict?," "How Does Technology Help Alternative Media?," and "Is It Advantageous to Utilize Alternative Media?" The political and moral implications to the Fifth Estate and its expansion are vast and ever-changing, especially as the Internet continues to grow in a way that is difficult to govern on both national and international levels.

CHAPTER 1

What Potential Does Alternative Media Have to Influence Society?

Chapter Preface

The rapid expansion of the Internet and the digital press has allowed the alternative media to have a greater foothold in society. Since the alternative media centers much of its efforts on keeping the traditional media in check by reporting on little-covered stories that have significant impacts on media consumers, it has had significant influence on major events, including the 2016 United State presidential election. But with this expansion of coverage comes incidents like "Pizzagate" or other "fake news" stories that went viral and are incorrectly treated as fact by certain corners of mainstream outlets. Additionally, the expansion of the alternative press has led to the vilification of elements of the free media, both traditional and alternative, which makes media consumers uncertain of whom and what they should believe at best, or at worst, completely misinformed.

There is very little consensus concerning how much influence the spread of fake news has on new forms of media. Facebook's Mark Zuckerberg claims that only 1 percent of stories found in people's news feeds could be considered fake news. But since more and more people use social media outlets and the Internet as their primary form of news, it is growing more difficult for people to ascertain what is factual and what is fake. And there is even less consensus on how to combat the spread of fake news and inaccuracy in all forms of media. With the CIA and NSA concluding that Russia did take efforts to undermine American democracy by assisting Donald Trump and the Republican Party, especially by utilizing fake news, the concerns about accuracy and transparency in the media continue to grow. With the mainstream media utilizing terms like "post-truth" and "alternative facts," it is difficult for the average media consumer to ascertain the accuracy of statements made by members of both the traditional media and even the US government.

The following chapter additionally covers the rapid growth of the alternative media, which was triggered by the rise of Julian Assange's website WikiLeaks, and the subsequent releases of classified government information and diplomatic cables from multiple countries. These actions and the actions of hacktivist organizations like Anonymous, which claim that they do not aim to cause damage but want to bring more light to political and social causes, use the Internet and digital media in a way that governments are not currently equipped to handle or contain, allowing for greater transparency between governments and their people, for better or for worse.

| *"Google's Safe Browsing List translates into the blocking of websites which allegedly contain malware."*

Google's Safe Browsing List Is Censoring Alternative Media

Christof Lehmann

In the following viewpoint, Christof Lehmann claims that there has been a concerted effort from the US government to censor and target members of the independent media. By using close relationships with heads of companies like Google, Apple, and Microsoft, the United States—specifically the NSA—is cracking down on small companies, including web-hosting institutions that rely on cooperation and partnerships for their economic survival, which may unfairly hide stories that are critical of the US government. With the US government potentially falsely claiming that independent media entities like the Drudge Report and Infowars contain malware, it may be unfairly defaming independent media and throttling the free press. Lehmann is an independent political consultant on conflict and conflict resolution and the founder and editor in chief of nsnbc international.

"Censorship Alert: The Alternative Media Getting Harassed by the NSA," by Christof Lehmann, *New Eastern Outlook*, December 10, 2014. Reprinted by permission.

As you read, consider the following questions:

1. According to the author, what are the consequences for "independent" media outlets should these outlets be flagged on Google's Safe Browsing List?
2. In the viewpoint, the author notes the close relationship between the chief of the NSA and heads of companies like Google, Apple, and Microsoft. What impact does this relationship have on the free and alternative press?
3. What is "soft censorship"?

Google's Safe Browsing List that blocks websites and flags them as containing malware is increasingly used as mechanism for the censoring of independent media and the falsification of history. It is an alarming development that, left unchallenged, puts the survival of any independent newspaper, blog, TV or radio station at risk. Over the past months the list has apparently been used to target websites critical of U.S.' involvement in the wars in the Middle East, U.S.' involvement in Ukraine and independent media who are publishing material that is critical of Zionism.

Google's Safe Browsing List translates into the blocking of websites which allegedly contain malware. Instead of showing the website one is presented with a red-colored Google page that warns that the URL in question has been blocked because it contains malware. Ultimately, being flagged on the list can also result in the removal of the flagged websites from Google's search engine. Being flagged, blocked or removed from search engines can have devastating results for independent journalists and media who are struggling to finance investigative journalism, rather than regurgitating alternative versions of Reuters and other major news agencies. The targeting of independent media and journalists is especially noteworthy when one considers Google's close cooperation with the United States' National Security Agency (NSA).

Incestuous Relationships between Google, Apple, Microsoft, their Subsidiaries, and the NSA

Google's close cooperation with the NSA is a well-documented fact. An article from May 7, entitled "Is Google in cahoots with the NSA? Email leak reveals close relationship", published in Tech Times, reveals that the close cooperation between Google and the NSA was documented long before NSA whistleblower Edward Snowden told the world what most who cared to investigate already knew. The article quotes emails between NSA Director Gen. Keith Alexander and Google executives Sergey Brin and Eric Schmidt from 2011 and 2012. Tech Times states:

> In the mails, the Google executives sound friendly and cooperative. Alexander's emails hint at the importance of Google's participation in refinement, engineering and deployment of solutions to cyber threats.

The article also details the fact that the NSA chief had invited CEOs of key companies including Google, Apple, and Microsoft to classified briefings. What is important about these three key corporations cooperation with the NSA is that they are economically interrelated with most other, commercial Internet providers, including web-hosting companies, firms which provide Internet security products, as well as advertising companies who sell advertising on everything from blogs over smaller independent media to major corporate newspapers. The following are recent examples, which demonstrate how this incestuous relationship translates into the targeting of independent media, censorship and the falsification of history.

October 6, nsnbc received an e-mail from the Internet security provider SiteLock, warning that there was a serious malware issue pertaining to some articles published in nsnbc. SiteLock stressed that the issue had to be resolved within 72 hours if nsnbc international wanted to avoid being added to Google's Safe Browsing List and have the site withdrawn from nsnbc's web-host, which among many other web hosts is a business partner of Site Lock.

So what was the alleged threat and what is the real threat—to the USA?

A full security scan conducted by nsnbc with the newspaper's own security software revealed that several articles had been flagged as containing malware. Among them were six articles which had been published on the renown independent on-line newspaper Voltairenet. All of the articles which had been flagged as containing malware dealt with illegal U.S. Involvement in the Syria war and illegal U.S. Involvement in Ukraine.

Another article that was flagged as containing malware was the article "Palestine Israel History and Theirstory". The article was originally published in nsnbc and it has been republished in numerous other independent media, including the International Middle East Media Center (IMEMC), Sabbah Report, and about 100 independent blogs. The reason why this particular article was flagged as containing malware was that it contained a link to the publication "Der Ewige Jude" a racist, supremacist propaganda book published by the German Nazi Party during WWII. The article documents the systematic dehumanization of Arabs by Zionists and Hollywood, and compares the dehumanization with that Nazis practiced against Jews and Slavic people.

Our scan further revealed that an article by the Bangkok based, independent analyst, editor of LandDestroyer Report, and contributor to New Eastern Outlook, nsnbc and others, Tony Cartalucci, also was on the list of flagged articles. The article is entitled "America's Nazis in Kiev: "Russians are Subhuman". The article was published in New Eastern Outlook, and was republished in LandDestroyer and nsnbc international. Tony Cartalucci demonstrates the Nazi ideology of post-coup Ukrainian PM Arseny Yatzenyuk by quoting Yatzenyuk, and referring to the Nazi pamphlet "Der Untermensch", so one could understand that Yatzenyuk's quote directly reflects the racist and supremacist ideology that was spread in "Der Untermensch", which translates into "The Subhuman". Also here, nsnbc has to remove the URL to the pamphlet and any media that continues carrying the URL risks, knowingly or not, to be added to Google's "Safe Browsing List" to have the newspaper's, journal's or blogs website flagged as containing malware, and to be removed or at the very least significantly down-graded in Google's search engine.

The real threat is, in other words, the threat that direct U.S. Collaboration with terrorists in Syria and Nazis in Ukraine is disclosed to a growing number of readers who have become suspicious about the accuracy of mainstream, corporate, state and foundation funded media. nsnbc did not respond to the initial SiteLock email but received a second email from SiteLock, late at night on October 8. In the mail SiteLock's Website Security Consultant Hubert Robinson wrote:

> My name is Hugh with SiteLock I recently left you a message regarding the status of your web domain, nsnbc.me During a recent SiteLock security scan of your website, malware was detected that could jeopardize the safety of your website and your data. I wanted to reach out before Google blacklist the site or before your Hosting provider pulls the site down for being infected. .... Please contact me immediately at 602-753-3929, so that I can help you secure your website as soon as possible.

We conducted an additional security scan with nsnbc's own software and didn't identify additional "threats", other than those articles by Voltairenet, nsnbc, LandDestroyer Report and New Eastern Outlook which documented U.S.' collaboration with wanted Al-Qaeda terrorists in Syria and Iraq, the article that documented that Zionist and Nazi ideology in large parts are identical, and the article which disclosed the Nazi ideology of Ukrainian PM Arseny Yatzenyuk whom the U.S.' administrations attempt to pass off as "house trained".

After nsnbc had de-activated the links to the URLs which allegedly contain malware, nsnbc wrote three mails to SiteLock's Website Security Consultant Huge Grant, asking, among others, whether they could be more specific about which malware the flagged sites allegedly contained. We also asked whether SiteLock has a direct or indirect corporate partnership with Google, and for the name and contact details of SiteLock's CEO. SiteLock failed to respond. SiteLock also failed to inform nsnbc whether the deactivation of the flagged URL's was "sufficient" or whether they perceived other "threats" to our "security".

Infecting Independent Media with Malware via Ad Companies

In February 2013, nsnbc was suddenly taken off-line and flagged as containing malware by Google's Safe Browsing List. The incident occurred about 20 minutes after nsnbc published an article entitled "US' Victoria Nuland about Ukraine ´F*** the EU`". The article contained a covertly recorded and leaked phone conversation between the U.S. State Department's Victoria Nuland and U.S. Ambassador to Ukraine Geoffrey Pyatt. The conversation revealed that the U.S.' was directly involved in the micro-management of the coup d'état in Ukraine.

nsnbc immediately investigated the reason for the closure of the newspaper's website. The result of the investigation was that nsnbc' at that time advertising partner, MadAdsMedia, which is heavily economically dependent on cooperation with Google and Google's AdSense, had inserted an ad that contained a Java Script with malware. Contacting MadAdsMedia resulted in their consultant explaining that they were "terribly sorry for the incident and any inconvenience it had caused us, assured that they were removing the ad that contained malware and advised us how to contact Google to have the newspaper removed from Google's Safe Browsing List".

nsnbc contacted MadAdsMedia and politely asked whether they would be so kind to send us detailed information about which ad it was that had contained the malware, and documentation for who it was that had placed the malware, and on which websites. MadAdsMedia failed to respond to at least three polite reminders by email and several phone calls. What MadAdsMedia did, however, was to inform nsnbc that it had decided not to serve any ads to nsnbc any longer and that they had moved us to another company whom we could contact if we wanted. In practical terms, the incident translates into this:

A minor advertising company that is heavily dependent on serving ads via a partnership with Google denies to answer justified questions and responds to the audacity to continue asking them by withdrawing an independent newspaper's only source of income, from one day to the other, without prior notice.

Facebook's "Soft" Censorship?

On September 5, New Eastern Outlook contributor and editor of LandDestroyer, Tony Cartalucci, published an article entitled "Beware: Facebook's 'Soft Censorship'". Cartalucci stressed that LandDestroyer Report had maintained a Facebook page under the name Anthony Cartalucci since 2009. Many of the readers of LandDestroyer Report used Facebook as a means of accessing the LD Reports articles. Tony Cartalucci wrote:

> Today, Facebook, without prior warning or opportunity to appeal, decided that the Facebook account must be changed over to a page. By doing so, all those following my account no longer would receive updates, because of Facebook's "news feeds" filter.

Note that one of Tony Cartalucci's articles also was among those flagged by SiteLock as containing malware. Moreover, Tony Cartalucci's experience with Facebook's "soft censorship" as he described it, is not unprecedented. Two of nsnbc editor Christof Lehmann's Facebook accounts were closed or blocked by Facebook within a period of less than twelve months. The accounts were not only used personally, but as a basis for a nsnbc Facebook page—one of that type Facebook demanded that Tony Cartalucci should open.

Facebook's way of blocking these two accounts were simple. Facebook demanded that a large number of "friend's" profile photos were matched with the correct names of these "friends". Now, consider 1,000 "friends or followers", and many of them using anything but their own portrait as profile photo. It is needless to say that solving that "quiz" is impossible.

A Concerted U.S.' Effort to Censor, Target Independent Media Economically, Withdraw Their Reader Base, and Falsify History

Let us sum up some of the main issues. The incestuous relationship between the NSA and major corporations like Google, Apple, Facebook and Microsoft is a well-documented fact. Many of the smaller companies, including web-hosting companies, Internet security providers, and advertising companies are either in part owned by one of these major corporations or they are heavily dependent on cooperation and partnerships with them for their economic survival. nsnbc has already experienced being closed down and have its only source of income withdrawn from one day to the other. Others, including Voltairenet have regularly been flagged as containing malware. Media like New Eastern Outlook, IMEMC, and others risk being targeted in similar manner. Others whom Google and a U.S. Senate Hearing falsely accused of containing malware are The Drudge Report and Infowars. One can only guess how many of the smaller blogs, who are too small to raise alarm bells have been targeted. The conclusion is that the United States is engaged in an aggressive campaign that targets independent media and falsifies history. The question is, whether independent media have the political will to stand united and addressing the problem and in using the fact that they serve a growing part of, for example, the advertising market as leverage.

> "[T]he Department of Homeland
> Security and the Director of National
> Intelligence released a joint statement
> accusing Russia of interfering with
> the American election process."

WikiLeaks May Have Influenced the Presidential Election

Mary Louise Kelly

In the following viewpoint, Mary Louise Kelly discusses the announcement that the CIA made in late 2016 that Russia intervened in the 2016 US presidential election, potentially tipping it in Donald Trump's favor. The Department of Homeland Security and the director of National Intelligence issued a joint statement supporting the CIA's findings and that Russia hacked both Democratic organizations and the Republican National Committee's computer systems. The then-president elect's transition team disputed the reports and instead falsely asserted that Trump's margin of victory was one of the largest in US election history. Kelly is national security correspondent for NPR News.

"CIA Concludes Russian Interference Aimed to Elect Trump," by Mary Louise Kelly, NPR .org, December 10, 2016. Reprinted by permission.

As you read, consider the following questions:

1. Why did the CIA change its assessment of Russia's interference in the 2016 election?
2. What historical falsehood did Trump's team use to attempt to dispel the CIA's assessment?
3. Why does Senator Angus King say this information is important for future elections?

The CIA has concluded that Russia intervened in the 2016 election specifically to help Donald Trump win the presidency, a U.S. official has confirmed to NPR.

"Before, there was confidence about the fact that Russia interfered," the official says. "But there was low confidence on what the direction and intentionality of the interference was. Now they [the CIA] have come to the conclusion that Russia was trying to tip the election to Trump."

The official adds: "The reason the assessment changed is that new information became available" since Oct. 7, when the Department of Homeland Security and the Director of National Intelligence released a joint statement accusing Russia of interfering with the American election process.

The Washington Post first reported the CIA's new assessment on Friday.

In addition to hacking into Democratic organizations, Russians hacked the Republican National Committee's computer systems, according to a separate report from The New York Times—but they did not release any information that might have been retrieved from Republican networks.

"Intelligence agencies have identified individuals with connections to the Russian government who provided WikiLeaks with thousands of hacked emails from the Democratic National Committee and others, including Hillary Clinton's campaign chairman, according to U.S. officials," the *Post* reports. "Those officials described the individuals as actors known to the intelligence community and part of a wider Russian operation to boost Trump and hurt Clinton's chances."

Citing anonymous officials briefed on the issue, the *Post* says the CIA shared its findings with senators in a closed-door briefing last week, saying it was now "quite clear" that Russia's goal was to tip the presidency in Trump's favor:

> "It is the assessment of the intelligence community that Russia's goal here was to favor one candidate over the other, to help Trump get elected," said a senior U.S. official briefed on an intelligence presentation made to U.S. senators. "That's the consensus view."

In a previous assessment, CIA officials had thought Russians intervened with the intention of undermining Americans' electoral system, Adam Entous, one of the *Post* story's reporters, tells NPR's Scott Simon.

On Friday evening, the Trump transition team fired back with a statement dismissing the report of the agency's conclusion.

"These are the same people that said Saddam Hussein had weapons of mass destruction," the statement said. "The election ended a long time ago in one of the biggest Electoral College victories in history. It's now time to move on and 'Make America Great Again.'"

In fact, Trump's percentage of the electoral vote in the 2016 election ranks 46th among presidential election winners in U.S. history, according to factcheck.org.

Trump's claim is a reference to the CIA's flawed intelligence on Iraq, in the run-up to the U.S.-led invasion in 2003. The CIA and other spy agencies judged that Saddam Hussein had weapons of mass destruction—a judgment that proved to be false. While the leadership of the CIA has changed hands several times in the years since then, many intelligence officers and analysts who worked on the Iraq intelligence still serve at CIA and in other parts of the U.S. intelligence community.

But whether or not Trump's top officials acknowledge the report as a possible threat, the *Post*'s Adam Entous points out Trump will soon be in command of the intelligence agencies.

"I'm sure they're going to declassify some elements of the report and I'm sure there will be leaks," he adds, but the Obama administration can't disclose the full details of the case, because it would be "compromising what's known as 'sources and methods,' which would then make it harder for the CIA and the NSA and other spy agencies to get more information in the future."

Earlier Friday, President Obama ordered the intelligence community to conduct a "full review" of "malicious cyber activity" timed to U.S. elections, as we previously reported:

> In the 2016 election, U.S. intelligence officials charged that Russia had interfered. In early October, they released a strongly worded statement saying they were "confident that the Russian Government directed the recent compromises of e-mails from U.S. persons and institutions, including from U.S. political organizations." The statement went on to say "these thefts and disclosures are intended to interfere with the U.S. election process."

The U.S. official says that "there is a determination to do something" before the Obama administration leaves power. "It's still being discussed exactly what to do. And as we've said before, some of it you may see and some of it you will not."

Sen. Ron Wyden, a Democrat on the Senate Intelligence Committee, says the response from President-elect Donald Trump is "very misguided."

"When you have strong evidence that a foreign power has interfered with the American election, with American institutions, then what you do is keep digging. You get all the facts out," Wyden says. "You respond to the American people with the kind of information that they have a right to know."

He also advocates releasing more information on the cyberattacks.

Whistleblower or Hacktivist?

In what transparency advocates and defenders of free speech see as a troubling development, the Obama administration on Wednesday released a multi-agency "strategy"—designed to combat cyber-crime and foreign espionage—which makes unsettling comparisons to the work of the government and corporate whistleblower media outlet Wikileaks to criminal hacking syndicates.

"Disgruntled insiders [may leak] information about corporate trade secrets or critical U.S. technology to 'hacktivist' groups like WikiLeaks," the White House document warns, belying the well established fact that Wikileaks does not operate as a 'hacking' site but as a clearing house for leaked documents that acts as a media outlet more than anything else.

According to Wikileaks' own website, it describes itself as is "a not-for-profit media organization."

Its goal, the group states, "is to bring important news and information to the public. We provide an innovative, secure and anonymous way for sources to leak information to our journalists. One of our most important activities is to publish original source material alongside our news stories so readers and historians alike can see evidence of the truth."

The organization is listed under a description of hacktivists and even described as an example of a "hacktivist" organization. This is blatantly false and malicious because staffers of WikiLeaks are not known to have hacked into any businesses or organizations to obtain information. They are not even known to have solicited information from insiders. All information released has been the result of submissions from sources they are unable to identify because their submission system was setup to protect the identity of sources or the information has been personally handed over by a whistleblower, who publicly wanted to be identified as the source.

"US Government Conflates Media Outlet Wikileaks with Cyber-Criminals and 'Hacktivists," by Jon Queally, Common Dreams, February 21, 2013.

"I do believe there is important information that the American people have a right to know. It ought to be declassified promptly."

"It's very important that the American public knows what happened, not necessarily to re-litigate this election, but to look forward," says Sen. Angus King, an independent senator from Maine. "What worries me is the extent to which this is an ongoing pattern—which, by the way, is the Russians' pattern in other parts of the world.

"And is that going to be the case in our elections? Four years from now, are we going to have the Democrats, the Republicans, the independents and the Russians?" King asks. "I mean, this is very serious stuff."

> *"Leaking the content of US diplomatic cables caused dramatically harder reactions in different countries than any other of the earlier actions of WikiLeaks."*

"Principled Leaking" Might Rightly Lead to Extended Censorship and Data Surveillance

Päivikki Karhula

In the following viewpoint, Päivikki Karhula discusses the short history of WikiLeaks and the documents it released to the international community. Originally launched as a wiki site, it has since moved to a more traditional publication model where its texts are only edited by its editors. WikiLeaks was founded in 2006 by Chinese dissidents, journalists, mathematicians, and start-up company technologists from the United States, Taiwan, South Africa, Australia, and Europe. WikiLeaks' document releases have been considered polarizing, inciting an especially divided opinion among civil rights organizations in the United States. Karhula is chief information specialist, Electronic Resources Library at Parliament of Finland.

"What Is the Effect of WikiLeaks for Freedom of Information?" by Päivikki Karhula, IFLA, October 5, 2012. https://www.ifla.org/publications/what-is-the-effect-of-wikileaks-for-freedom-of-information. Licensed Under CC BY 4.0 International.

As you read, consider the following questions:

1. Why were the reactions to the leaks of US diplomatic cables harder than reactions from Wikileaks' actions in other countries?
2. Why are Wikileaks' actions a detriment to countries keeping peaceful international relations?
3. What is SHIELD?

What Do the Recent WikiLeaks Documents Address?

The most high-profile documents hosted by WikiLeaks are either US based documents or they focus on alleged US government misbehavior. Many of them relate to hidden war crimes or prisoner abuse. The following sections describe the content and value of leaked publications and public reactions on the leaks.

In March 2007 WikiLeaks published the US military's operating manual for the Guantanamo prison camp (Standard Operating Procedures for Camp Delta). The manual indicated that some prisoners were placed outside the areas which members from the International Committee of the Red Cross were allowed to visit. This was something the military has repeatedly denied.

In July 2010, WikiLeaks released *Afghan War Diary*, a compilation of more than 76,900 documents about the War in Afghanistan which were not previously available to the public. These documents indicated that the deaths of innocent civilians at the hands of international forces were covered up.

In October 2010, WikiLeaks released a package of almost 400,000 documents called the *Iraq War Logs* in coordination with major commercial media organizations. US officials confirmed that this was the largest leak of US military secrets in history. The "war logs" showed alleged evidence of torture that was ignored, and that there were more than 109,000 violent deaths between 2004 and 2009 including 66,081 civilians.[1]

On November 28th 2010, WikiLeaks began releasing US State Department diplomatic cables. The New York Times, Le

Monde, Der Spiegel, The Guardian and El Pais in co-operation with WikiLeaks published the first articles which revealed that over 250,000 confidential documents had been leaked to WikiLeaks. During the same night the first 219 documents of the diplomatic cables were published on the WikiLeaks website. According to WikiLeaks, all cables will be published during the coming months. By the 4th of December 2010 over 800 cables had been published.[2]

The diplomatic cables originated from Siprnet (Secret Internet Network), a closed network of the US Department of Defence. Over the past ten years US Embassies worldwide were plugged into Siprnet in an effort to increase information sharing. Documents were available on Siprnet for over 2 million people including all military staff. About 100,000 of the leaked cables were labeled "confidential", about 15.000 had the higher classification "secret", but there were no documents classified as "top secret" on the classification scale.[3]

Reactions to Diplomatic Cable Leaks

Leaking the content of US diplomatic cables caused dramatically harder reactions in different countries than any other of the earlier actions of WikiLeaks. It made also civil rights organizations reconsider their stand on WikiLeaks.

On December 6th US Attorney General Eric Holder announced that WikiLeaks was under criminal investigation and that there could be prosecutions of individuals for leaking classified documents. Julian Assange, director of WikiLeaks, was arrested 7th December 2010 in Britain and accused of sexual assaults in Sweden. However, he was released 16th December against bail for a home arrest. No charges due to the leaks have been filed so far against him.

WikiLeaks also became as a target of attacks and blocks. Immediately after the documents were published, a denial-of-service (DoS) attack was carried out against the WikiLeaks website. WikiLeaks was blocked by government organizations and service providers in China, UAE, Australia (on a black list), Switzerland (by a US service provider) and in the USA (from Federal Government staff, Library of Congress, Department of Education). Also, in California WikiLeaks was temporarily blocked from all DNS addresses after the cable leaks.

Several financial institutions, including Swiss PostFinance, PayPal, Bank of America, Visa and MasterCard, closed WikiLeaks' accounts shortly after the cables were published. These events were followed by DoS attacks against MasterCard and Visa which were organized by activists defending WikiLeaks. As a consequence of this attack Facebook and Twitter also closed the accounts and pages used by hackers.[4] As such, these reactions increased concerns about the tactics of WikiLeaks.

Direct censorship by blocking was not the only restrictive reaction against WikiLeaks. In USA university students as well as government staff and prospective employees were warned by the State Department not to read, print, comment on or make links to WikiLeaks.[5] The reasoning behind this warning was that the data in WikiLeaks is still officially held as classified.[6]

Government Reactions to WikiLeaks

US government reactions to WikiLeaks have hardened over time. Concerning Afghan War Diary, the Pentagon pressured WikiLeaks to return all documents. The Iraq War Logs leak in 2010 was condemned by the US and UK who suggested the disclosures put lives at risk.

The leak of the diplomatic cables in November 2010 naturally caused more reactions in different countries than any other items WikiLeaks had published, since it also touched sensitive political issues for different governments.

US policymakers have been both critical and supportive of WikiLeaks' actions. Secretary of State Hillary Clinton decried immediately the illegal publication of classified documents from government computers, and defended the need for "confidential space" for diplomatic conversations. In addition, she noted that people's lives could be endangered by confidential data disclosures.[7]

However, other governments' reactions were considerably milder concerning the possible impacts of the leaks. According to US Defense Secretary Robert Gates the leaks were embarrassing but he estimated that they would only have "modest" consequences for US foreign policy.[8]

German Interior Minister Thomas de Maizière described WikiLeaks as irritating and annoying for Germany, but not a threat. However, he also defended governments' position to hold secret information, saying "Governments also have to be able to communicate confidentially. Confidentiality and transparency are not mutually exclusive, but rather two sides of the same coin."[9]

In Finland politicians' reactions were controversial. Minister of Foreign Affairs, Alexande Stubb, described the leaks as regrettable and stated "I support transparency and public diplomacy. However, some information between states can be sensitive. This is certainly a difficult situation."[10]

Former Minister of Foreign Affairs, Erkki Tuomioja, emphasized that leaking of diplomatic cables was based on stealing of data and he saw WikiLeaks activities in this case as questionable. On the other hand, one member of the parliament, Annika Lapintie (Left Alliance) proposed a Nobel Prize for WikiLeaks.[11]

Divided Opinions Among Civil Rights Organizations

WikiLeaks has also become a dividing and controversial issue also among civil rights organizations. Many organizations agree on the undeniable value that WikiLeaks has had by indicating violations of human rights and civil liberties. According to Glenn Greenwald, lawyer and civil rights activist, the amount of corruption which WikiLeaks has exposed is unique in history and there is no other organization that comes close to WikiLeaks regarding exposures of misuse of power.[12]

Many civil right organizations have so far openly supported the work of WikiLeaks because of these reasons. The reasoning behind their support is based on the fair rules and justified functionality of democracy and civil society. If secrecy of administrative documents is used to cover government misbehavior, especially inhuman conditions and killing of people, there must be legal grounds to overcome formal borders of secrecy. This has seen as a justified way to protect democratic society and citizen against secret arbitrary government power.

However, the leaks of diplomatic cables made some civil rights organizations and activists back off with their full support for WikiLeaks. The Afghan War Diary leaks had already been harshly criticised by Reporters without Borders. They accused WikiLeaks of "incredible irresponsibility." Although they admitted that WikiLeaks "has in the past played a useful role" by exposing violations of human rights and civil liberties, the case of Afghan War Diary was to some extent different. WikiLeaks was accused of revealing the identity of hundreds of people who collaborated with the coalition in Afghanistan and making them vulnerable for further violence.[13]

Although there is largely an agreement about the value of leaked information, the strategies, tactics and mistakes of WikiLeaks have gained critics. It has also been questioned if the impact of the leaks will lead in an opposite direction than was expected: towards more secrecy and increasing restrictions. Stephen Aftergood, director of Federation of American Scientists Project on Government Secrecy comments: "It has invaded personal privacy. It has published libellous material. It has violated intellectual property rights. And above all, it has launched a sweeping attack not simply on corruption, but on secrecy itself. And I think that's both a strategic and a tactical error. It's a strategic error because some secrecy is perfectly legitimate and desirable. It's a tactical error because it has unleashed a furious response from the US government and other governments that I fear is likely to harm the interests of a lot of other people besides WikiLeaks who are concerned with open government. It may become harder to support protection for people who disclose and publish classified information after WikiLeaks."[14]

Altogether, debate on WikiLeaks has become very complex. There seems to be a pressure on taking sides for or against WikiLeaks or giving statements for them. However, it will require an analytic discussion to recognize both pros and cons in their activities.

It is somewhat difficult for civil society organizations to make clear statements for several reasons. Firstly, WikiLeaks' political activities have taken different shapes during last years and even many transparency activists are not behind all of them. While it is unquestionable that leaks about war crimes and prison violence have given valuable information for society, it is harder to judge the value of data from large amount of diplomatic cables.

It would require weighing an undeniable efficiency of WikiLeaks' actions and validity of concerns they have revealed against their provocative and questionable ways of political action. "There is an alternative mechanism for progress", suggested Stephen Aftergood, "So it's really not a question of WikiLeaks or nothing. It's a question of a smart, well-targeted approach or a reckless shotgun approach."[15]

Impact of the Cable Leaks on Intellectual Freedom

What is the possible impact of WikiLeaks? Is it going to increase or restore the space of free speech or advance transparency of public documents? Or is it going to have the opposite effect and make governments strengthen their restrictions and increase different forms of Internet censorship?

There are several valid concerns and evident signs about stricter legislation and more in depth surveillance practices which may find their grounds on WikiLeaks. Shortly after cable leaks three US senators (Ensign, Lieberman, Brown) introduced a bill aimed at stopping WikiLeaks by making it illegal to publish the names of military or intelligence community informants. According to Brown, The Securing Human Intelligence and Enforcing Lawful Dissemination Act (SHIELD) would prevent anyone from compromising national security in the future in a similar manner to WikiLeaks.[16]

Another bill under discussion would give the US government extended rights to wiretap all online communication and Internet traffic including foreign-based service providers. The wiretapping bill would also require software developers which enable peer-to-peer communication to redesign their service to allow interception.[17] Concerns have been raised if WikiLeaks is used to gain support for this legislation.[18]

In early December 2010 US senators Joe Lieberman and Dianne Feinstein invoked the 1917 Espionage Act and urged its use in prosecuting Julian Assange. Liebermann also extended his invocation to include the use of this Act to investigate the New York Times, which published WikiLeaks' diplomatic cables. Naomi Wolf, journalist and civil rights activists, warned about the consequences of this practice: "Assange, let us remember, is the New York Times in the parallel case of the Pentagon Papers, not Daniel Ellsberg; he is the publisher, not the one who revealed the classified information—then any outlet, any citizen, who discusses or addresses 'classified' information can be arrested on 'national security' grounds", concluded Wolf.[19]

Another a crucial issue is the protection of sources. What will happen to journalists' rights to publish leaked information? US lawyer and civil rights activist Glenn Greenwald condenses this concern soundly: "Put simply, there is no intellectually coherent way to distinguish what WikiLeaks has done with these diplomatic cables with what newspapers around the world did in this case and what they do constantly: namely, receive and then publish classified information without authorization".[20]

The consequences of losing a right to protect sources may lead to extreme transparency, but does it lead to the kind of transparency which would support democracy and civil society? American journalist, Claire Berlinski reveals the faulty logic of this kind of philosophy in her statement: "The hypocrisy and double-standard of journalists, in particular, who fail to understand why the government must sometimes protect its sources of information is mind-blowing. Journalists, of all people, should understand this better than anyone else. Many sources would lose their jobs, their reputations, their liberty or their lives for talking to journalists on the record. If the people who spoke to us didn't think we could keep their names out of the story, they would never open their mouths again. Would that make the world more transparent?"[21]

Library and Information Field and WikiLeaks

According to the ALA (American Library Association), WikiLeaks relates to many policy issues including access to government information, censorship and the blocking of web sites, government secrecy and the over-classification of government information, treatment of whistleblowers, government transparency and the legalities surrounding classified information. Presently, it looks like WikiLeaks has raised dozens of political and legal questions which will take time to respond to.[22]

Also, in the library field there have been controversial approaches to WikiLeaks. Library of Congress have blocked access to WikiLeaks, which has raised a vivid debate on censorship among libraries.[23] Consequently, ALA has compiled a proposal for a resolution to support accessibility to WikiLeaks and library associations in other countries are considering the same.[24]

From FAIFE's point of view it would be valuable to focus on the direct and indirect censorship effects of WikiLeaks in different countries, organizations and libraries. However, as indicated, WikiLeaks may also be used as a case to support such new bills, surveillance practices and use of technologies which extend capabilities of censorship and data surveillance. Unfortunately, there is not yet much evidence of the development trend towards another direction: to strengthen transparency and increase the space for freedom of speech within the aftermath of WikiLeaks.

Endnotes
1. BBC. Wikileaks: Iraq war logs 'reveal truth about conflict. BBC News (bbc.co.uk), 23.10.2010
2. United States Diplomatic Cable Leaks. Wikipedia
3. United States Diplomatic Cable Leaks. Wikipedia

4. The Economist, The War on Wikileaks. Economist.com, 9.12.2010

5. Wikipedia (English). Wikileaks

6. Fishman, Rob, State Department To Columbia University Students: DO NOT Discuss WikiLeaks On Facebook. Twitter, The Huffington Post (huffingtonpost.com), 6.12.2010.

7. Jones, Barbara, Wikileaks and its relationship to ALA.

8. Whitlock, Craig, Gates: Warnings of WikiLeaks fallout overblown. The Washington Post (voices.washingtonpost.com), 30.11.2010.

9. Stark, Holger & Rosenbach, Marcel, WikiLeaks Is Annoying, But Not a Threat. Spiegel Online, 20.12.2010

10. YLE. Finland Surfaces in Wikileaks Exposé. YLE.fi, 29.11.2010

11. Wikipedia (Finnish). Wikileaks

12. Is WikiLeaks' Julian Assange a Hero? Glenn Greenwald Debates Steven Aftergood of Secrecy News / Democracy Now (Video & transcript), 3.12.2010

13. Siddique, Haroon, Press freedom group joins condemnation of WikiLeaks' war logs. The Guardian (guardian.co.uk), 13.8.2010.

14. Is WikiLeaks' Julian Assange a Hero? Glenn Greenwald Debates Steven Aftergood of Secrecy News / Democracy Now (Video & transcript), 3.12.2010

15. Is WikiLeaks' Julian Assange a Hero? Glenn Greenwald Debates Steven Aftergood of Secrecy News / Democracy Now (Video & transcript), 3.12.2010

16. Nagesh, Gautham, Senators unveil anti-WikiLeaks bill. The Hill (thehill.com), 3.12.2010

17. Savage, Charlie, U.S. tries to make it easier to wiretap the Internet. The New York Times (nytimes.com), 27.9.2010.

18. Is The US Response To Wikileaks Really About Overhyping Online Threats To Pass New Laws?, Techdirt, 13.12.2010.

19. Wolf, Naomi, Espionage Act: How the Government Can Engage in Serious Aggression Against the People of the United States, The Huffington Post (huffingtonpost.com), 10.12.2010.

20. Greenwald, Glenn, Attempts to prosecute WikiLeaks endanger press freedoms. Salon (salon.com), 14.12.2010.

21. Pilon, Roger, Keeping WikiLeaks in perspective. Cato @ Liberty (cato-at-liberty.org), 6.12.2010

22. Jones, Barbara, Wikileaks and its relationship to ALA

23. Why the Library of Congress Is Blocking Wikileaks

24. Revised version: Resolution in Support of WikiLeaks (12/29/10)]

"Hacktivists are almost like vigilantes. They're looking to disrupt."

Hacktivists Are Hacking for a Cause

Jenni Bergal

In the following viewpoint, Jenni Bergal discusses the recent emergence of "hacktivists," or online activists that blend hacking and activism for a political social cause. Hacktivism has been gaining more and more traction in recent years, bringing added attention to the Flint water crisis, response to North Carolina's controversial state law attacking transgender people, the city of Baltimore's decision not to indict those involved with Freddie Gray's death while in police custody, and more. There is a continued debate about whether hacktivism is truly a harmless action or if these attacks will grow and cause more damage with the strength of groups like Anonymous. Bergal is an award-winning journalist who covers the business of government for Stateline.

As you read, consider the following questions:

1. What is hacktivism?
2. How many hacktivist incidents were recorded in 2015 and 2016?
3. Why are the actions of hacktivist groups so damaging to public trust?

"Hacktivists' Increasingly Target Local and State Government Computers," by Jenni Bergal ©The Pew Charitable Trusts, January 10, 2017. Reprinted by permission.

E arly last year, hackers launched a cyberattack against the state of Michigan's main website to draw attention to the Flint water crisis. In May, they targeted North Carolina government websites to protest a controversial state law requiring transgender people to use bathrooms that match the sex on their birth certificate. And in July, they took aim at the city of Baton Rouge's website after the fatal police shooting of a black man.

It's called "hacktivism," a blend of hacking and activism for a political or social cause, and state and local governments are increasingly finding themselves targets. Unlike cyber criminals who hack into computer networks to steal data for the cash, most hacktivists aren't doing it for the dollars. They're individuals or groups of hackers who band together and see themselves as fighting injustice.

"It's digital disobedience. It's hacking for a cause," said Dan Lohrmann, chief security officer for Security Mentor, a national security training firm that works with states.

Hacktivists have gone after everyone from foreign governments and corporations to drug dealers and pedophiles. Police departments, hospitals, small towns, big cities and states also have come under attack. Online activists have successfully frozen government servers, defaced websites, and hacked into data or email and released it online.

"Some take this as being harmless and think it's another form of protest," said Doug Robinson, executive director of the National Association of State Chief Information Officers (NASCIO). "But it can be highly disruptive. It's criminal trespassing."

Robinson said he has seen a "significant growth" in the number and severity of hacktivist attacks on state and local governments in the past five years. For the public, it can mean being unable to log on to government websites to get information or conduct business. And for taxpayers, it can mean having to pick up the tab for staff time and additional technology needed to combat such attacks.

When Baltimore was rocked by protests over Freddie Gray's death from injuries sustained while in police custody in April

2015, for example, hacktivists knocked out the city's main website that gives the public information about government services for at least 16 hours.

"Hacktivists are almost like vigilantes. They're looking to disrupt," said Brian Calkin, a vice president of the Multi-State Information Sharing and Analysis Center, a federally funded group that tracks cybersecurity issues for states and local governments.

Calkin said his group tracked 65 hacktivist incidents involving state and local governments in 2015; the number jumped to 160 last year. And a 2014 survey of state information technology security officials listed hacktivism as one of their top three cyber concerns.

"Hacktivism is becoming more and more of a serious issue," said Srini Subramanian, a state cybersecurity principal at the consulting firm Deloitte & Touche LLP.

Subramanian said hacktivists don't just want to disrupt services; they also want to undermine public trust. "That is what is going to move the hacktivists to continue to do this."

Hacktivist Attacks

Hacktivists are an amorphous group. While some may be individuals unhappy with a perceived social injustice, many are linked to loosely associated networks such as Anonymous, a major hacktivist group responsible for attacking government, corporate and religious websites.

Anonymous describes itself on its website as a "relatively small vigilante cyber group" that has "expanded and transformed into a continuation of the Civil-Rights movement."

Hacktivists use various tools: Sometimes, they hack into private email or confidential records and make them public. Sometimes, they compile personal information about targets such as police officers from the internet or government record breaches and post it online, which is called "doxing" (a derivative of "docs," slang for documents). The information can include a person's home address, phone number and even the names of his children. Hacktivists see it as transparency; security experts see it as harassment.

Often, hacktivists launch "denial-of-service" attacks, in which they try to knock a website offline by flooding it with traffic. To do that, they take control of a large group of computers—sometimes tens of thousands or more—using malware that unsuspecting people have launched on their home or office computers by clicking on an email with an attachment or a link to a website. The hacktivists then control the so-called "zombie" computers and direct them to bombard a specific website with traffic at the same time, causing it to freeze.

"A given website can only handle so many visitors," Calkin said. "When you exceed that number, the server will crash. When you keep that attack up, there's no way to recover it while it's happening."

If a government computer system doesn't have the protections to block such attacks, a website can be knocked offline anywhere from several minutes to 24 hours or longer.

Experts generally don't consider cyber espionage by foreign governments or intelligence agencies to be hacktivism. But some do include groups such as WikiLeaks, an international organization that publishes secret or classified information, some of which has been hacked by others with political or social agendas.

"Hacktivism isn't just about crashing systems or bringing down websites," Lohrmann said. "It's hacking to achieve the ends of social or political causes. It could be stealing information or publishing information to embarrass or discredit people."

Some hacktivist attacks have been successful; others haven't.

In North Carolina, the May attacks over the transgender bathroom law were a bust because the state's main websites continued to operate normally during and after the attacks, said Katie Diefes, a state Department of Information Technology spokeswoman. The only websites affected were some older ones that simply redirected users to the main ones.

Hacktivists were more successful when they sounded off against the fatal police shooting of Michael Brown, an unarmed black teenager, Aug. 9, 2014, in Ferguson, Missouri, which prompted protests and riots.

Within a week of Brown's death, Anonymous began its assault, using denial of service tactics and doxing high-level state, local and law enforcement officials, said Michael Roling, the state's chief information security officer. The group targeted the state's main website as well as those of the revenue and public safety departments.

While IT staff was quick to launch its defenses and help blunt the attacks, Roling said state websites suffered brief outages in August 2014 and again three months later, after a grand jury decided not to indict the officer who shot Brown. "Fortunately, we were able to get controls in place before they had the opportunity to do damage or affect the delivery of state services," he said.

But Roling noted that his team worked for weeks defending the state's computer network against hacktivists. And it came at a cost: at least $150,000 for services to protect the network.

"We have the resources but we've seen some local governments across the country that don't have the funding or have no way of quickly procuring services to fight these attacks, and their services are knocked offline," Roling said.

Fending Off Attacks

Cybersecurity experts warn that state and local governments need to prepare to fight all sorts of online attacks, including those by cyber activists. Calkin said his group recommends that if government computer systems aren't equipped to handle hacktivist attacks, officials should work with their internet providers to install programs that help block illegitimate web traffic.

Or they can turn to global cybersecurity companies that offer services to combat massive assaults and scrub out "bad" traffic headed toward websites while keeping "good" traffic.

That's what Minnesota did, said Christopher Buse, the state's chief information security officer. "We're seeing more of these attacks than ever," he said. "They're bigger and they're becoming more complex and more costly to defend."

NASCIO's Robinson agrees states should step up their game and make sure they have the tools to thwart hacktivist assaults. But he admits it's hard to fight a threat that can come from anywhere at any time and for any reason.

Robinson also worries that as hacktivism gets more sophisticated, the consequences could become more serious. Instead of potentially affecting citizen services such as revenue collection or driver's license renewals for a brief period, he said hacktivists could do far greater damage by knocking out the electric grid, water systems or other utilities.

"We are all vulnerable, and hacktivism is going to continue as long as we have these crises or events where political activists want to make a statement, whether it's a police shooting or a city's decision to remove camps for the homeless."

Periodical and Internet Sources Bibliography

The following articles have been selected to supplement the diverse views presented in this chapter.

Hunt Allcott and Matthew Gentzkow, "Social Media and Fake News in the 2016 Election," *Journal of Economic Perspectives*, January 2017. https://web.stanford.edu/~gentzkow/research/fakenews.pdf.

Nayef Al-Rodhan, "Post-Truth Politics, the Fifth Estate and the Securization of Fake News," Global Policy, June 7, 2017. http://www.globalpolicyjournal.com/blog/07/06/2017/post-truth-politics-fifth-estate-and-securitization-fake-news.

Richard Edelman, "The Rise of the Fifth Estate—Speech," Edelman.com, December 5, 2016. http://www.edelman.com/post/richard-edelman-rise-of-fifth-estate-speech/.

Glenn Greenwald, "Is WikiLeaks' Julian Assange a Hero? Glenn Greenwald Debates Steven Aftergood of Secrecy News," Democracy Now!, December 3, 2010. https://www.democracynow.org/2010/12/3/is_wikileaks_julian_assange_a_hero.

John Herrman, "Online, Everything Is Alternative Media," *New York Times*, November 10, 2016. https://www.nytimes.com/2016/11/11/business/media/online-everything-is-alternative-media.html?mcubz=0.

Gautham Nagesh, "Senators Unveil Anti-WikiLeaks Bill," The Hill, December 7, 2010. http://thehill.com/policy/technology/131885-senators-unveil-anti-wikileaks-legislation.

Pew, "The Role of News on Facebook", Pew Research Center, October 24, 2013. http://www.journalism.org/2013/10/24/the-role-of-news-on-facebook/.

James Vincent, "Artificial Intelligence Is Going to Make It Easier than Ever to Fake Images and Video," The Verge, December 20, 2016. https://www.theverge.com/2016/12/20/14022958/ai-image-manipulation-creation-fakes-audio-video.

OPPOSING
VIEWPOINTS®
SERIES

CHAPTER 2

How Does Alternative Media Enable Extremist Civil Conflict?

Chapter Preface

T he rapid expansion of alternative media movements around the world not only allows for a greater transparency between the government and its citizens, but it also allows for greater civil conflict, especially in countries where the rights of the free press are not guaranteed. But when the mainstream media's approach toward covering terrorism and counterterrorism needs work, the alternative media steps in to attempt to answer why people are driven into the arms of such violent groups.

Since many of these violent groups currently have taken root in the Middle East and are or have been at one point influenced or funded by outside governments, including the United States, what can be done to counter violent extremism, especially when its origins can be traced to the West? If western governments attempt to spread democracy through autocratic countries, how can they ensure that what has happened will not happen again? It will take international, global action to discredit the spread of radical narratives and support the openness and awareness of what the tenants of Islam actually are, not the falsehoods perpetuated by both the extremist groups that claim to be a part of Islam or the mainstream media, which does not do enough to differentiate the extreme view from the truth behind the religion.

There is no one-size-fits-all theory behind what radicalizes a group, what turns a group of people with extreme views into the threatening forces that media consumers see on the news. They may come from similar causes, similar situations that all lead to the same likely conclusion, but with the rise of these groups comes the understanding of what it means to be radical or a violent radical. Without the understanding of that distinction, it is difficult to stop them.

Additionally, the focus of this chapter turns to the overall scope of literacy, especially media literacy, and the younger set of voters who are still in college and are developing their political and global perspectives. Studies that focus on college-age voters must rely on nontraditional survey methods in order to understand the overall scope of how media influences these votes and how they seek and encounter political-based news. With the advent of the Internet and the rapid expansion of digital media, traditional methods of influencing media consumers are no longer enough to shape the results of a political election.

| "*You don't want violent extremism? Don't fund it.*"

The Language of Moral Panic: "Radicalization" vs. "Extremism"

Ben Debney

In the following viewpoint, Ben Debney discusses the inherently problematic approaches taken by mainstream counterterrorist groups. Debney points out the history of the Islamic State, which traces back to al-Qaeda, which itself grew out of CIA funding and training of the mujahideen during the Soviet invasion of Afghanistan. If these Islamic extremist groups rise from the ashes of US funding, can they be considered radical if they do not fit the definition also stated in this viewpoint? These archconservatives feel that the status quo doesn't go far enough to undermine individual autonomy, but to dismantle such organizations, people must understand what drives some into the arms of such violent extremists. Debney is a PhD candidate in international relations at Deakin University, Burwood, Melbourne. He is studying moral panics and the political economy of scapegoating.

"The Language of Moral Panic: 'Radicalization' vs. 'Extremism,'" by Ben Debney, First appeared on Counterpunch.org, December 14, 2015. Reprinted by permission.

As you read, consider the following questions:

1. What does the author consider to be the differences between archconservatives and radicals?
2. Is the Islamic State any more politically radical than the United States' GOP, according to the viewpoint?
3. Why do people fall into the arms of violent extremism?

The extraordinary brutality and reactionary nihilism of fundamentalist groups like Islamic State is beyond doubt. In the face of the heinous acts of such groups, mainstream counter terrorist beyond doubt. In the face of the heinous acts of such groups, mainstream counter terrorist narratives arising from the Terror Scare present deradicalisation as an imperative part of addressing the problem. Are radicalism and extremism however the same thing?

Mainstream counter-terrorist responses treat them as though they are. This approach is profoundly problematic for actually dealing with violent extremism insofar as it conflates radical opposition to things as they are with the extremist responses chosen as a result. The two are and remain two separate things and no good reason exists to assume otherwise.

In reality the only good reason for doing so is to further the goals of the Terror Scare, the moral panic over terrorism, which renders the institutions and ideologies represented by the status quo as cause and cure of the same problem.

By tarnishing radical opposition to things as they are with the extremist responses chosen, the moral entrepreneurs of Terror Scare narratives can continue to do so by adopting an attitude of militant ignorance towards facts associated with the phenomenon of terrorism and violent extremism for which they are the cause (as well as the cure).

One such fact is the basic reason why Islamic State exists in the first place, which is because of long-term intervention by the United States and its Western allies in the affairs of Middle Eastern countries for most of the last century. Al Qaeda grew out of CIA funding and training of the Mujahadeen during the Soviet invasion of Afghanistan; Islamic State is the resurgent version of Al Qaeda in Iraq. You don't want violent extremism? Don't fund it.

Another such fact is that Islamic State are arch-conservatives; they are no more politically radical than the GOP (to the extent that the GOP is not radically reactionary at least). To conflate the cultish banditry of Islamic State with radical rebellion against the status quo is to purposely misrepresent its nature and goals for purposes that have nothing to do with preventing violent extremism.

The differences between the two couldn't be clearer. For the archconservatives of Islamic State, the status quo is unsatisfactory because it doesn't go far enough in undermining individual autonomy in the name of rendering its victims slaves to a fascist theocracy.

To radicals on the other hand, the status quo is unsatisfactory because it doesn't go far enough in promoting such autonomy so that we might enjoy control over the conditions of our own work and lives. Not only could the two outlooks not be more different; they are literally at opposite poles of the political compass (see politicalcompass.org).

We should hardly need to insult anyone's intelligence by spelling out what the political establishment might have to gain by associating radical rebellion with violent extremism.

And yet they do. Obama's 'Strategic Implementation Plan For Empowering Local Partners To Prevent Violent Extremism In The United States' of December 2011 speaks nowhere of addressing the reasons why people might be upset with, say, the pre-emptive invasion of Iraq, or the brutal treatment of Palestinians under Israeli occupation. Instead, their focus is on

1) enhancing engagement with and support to local communities that may be targeted by violent extremists; (2) building government and law enforcement expertise for preventing violent extremism; and (3) countering violent extremist propaganda while promoting our ideals.[1]

The National Center on Counterterrorism elaborates on these goals, noting of the third in particular that 'We must actively and aggressively counter the range of ideologies violent extremists employ to radicalize and recruit individuals by challenging justifications for violence and by actively promoting the unifying and inclusive vision of our American ideals.'[2]

The concern here is not to be with trying to understand what drives people into the arms of violent extremists and what their grievances are, but with reasserting American ideals—whatever those who conflate radicalism and extremism happen to decide they are. Should there be any wonder that the non-state form of terrorism that Terror Scare narratives treat as the only version in existence continues?

Others to their credit make somewhat more of an attempt to address root causes. Shiraz Maher, Senior Research Fellow at International Centre for the Study of Radicalisation, acknowledges at least that 'when Mohammad Sidique Khan led the 7/7 London terrorist attacks almost a decade ago, he said his actions were in retaliation for "the bombing, gassing, imprisonment and torture of my people."[3]

Maher's analysis of radicalization is fascinating if for no other reason than because he points out the apparent paradox stemming from the fact that 'Khan was killing his own people, the ordinary citizen-stranger commuting to work, when he detonated his bomb on the London underground.' Mahar bristles in response against Khan's claim that 'he identified with the citizens of Iraq —a country he had not even travelled to and whose language he could not speak?'

For Maher the problem is one of identification, the fact that Mohammad Sidique Khan identified with the victims of an act of illegal and immoral military aggression—as did millions of other people in the West who protested the invasion of Iraq.

If Khan's identification with the victims of Western aggression was a problem, then presumably that of millions of protesters, none of whom had been to Iraq or could speak Arabic either, must be as well. Naturally Mahar doesn't follow through with his logic to that conclusion, but that is where it must inevitably end for approaches to counter-terrorism built on the dominant narratives of the Terror Scare.

Without distinguishing between grievances and the nature of the responses chosen to address them, such approaches, those that render the West cause and cure of the same problem, must inevitably become an excuse for blame shifting and a continuing refusal to address vital social problems.

This is particularly true to the extent that they set a precedent via those who make destructive choices in their responses to those who make constructive ones. To continue the myth that grievances against the status quo ultimately result in violent extremism is to whittle away at what remains of individual freedoms in the name of defending them, which at the end of the day is exactly what violent extremists are after irrespective of whether they're in Iraq or Washington.

Notes

1. https://www.whitehouse.gov/sites/default/files/sip-final.pdf

2. http://www.nctc.gov/site/technical/radicalization.html

3. http://icsr.info/2015/06/icsr-insight-roots-radicalisation-identity-stupid/

> *"A global venture can target audiences through multiple avenues, maximizing efforts to discredit radical narratives."*

Alternative Narratives Can Counter Extremist Messaging

Ed Husain

In the following viewpoint, Ed Husain poses the idea for a global effort to counter violent extremism in the Middle East. The effort would require a centralized body that can lend legitimacy to the group, and based on American and Turkish cooperation at the Global Counterterrorism Forum, the United States should establish Turkey as this leader. The central goal of these efforts is to support initiatives that would maximize efforts to discredit radical narratives and support openness and awareness to the tenants of Islam, not the distorted propaganda perpetuated by extremist groups. Husain is adjunct senior fellow for Middle Eastern studies at the Council on Foreign Relations.

"A Global Venture to Counter Violent Extremism," by Ed Husain, Council on Foreign Relations, September 9, 2013. Reprinted by permission.

As you read, consider the following questions:

1. According to the viewpoint, where are extremist groups' ideological affiliates founded?
2. What is the meaning of the word *umma*, and what has the meaning been twisted into?
3. What monetary and time commitments does the author estimate the global fund would require?

The rise of Islamist radicalism continues to threaten U.S. interests in the greater Middle East. Last year's attacks on U.S. embassies, instability in the aftermath of the Arab uprisings, and an increase in political activism among Salafist movements are all cause for concern. In Pakistan, extremist networks use U.S. drone strikes and the killing of Osama bin Laden to rally people to their cause. Although Muslim organizations in the Middle East, Pakistan, Indonesia, and Europe have had some success countering violent extremism (CVE), these groups desperately need financial assistance to continue their work. The United States should address this funding gap. By using the existing Global Counterterrorism Forum (GCTF), founded by the U.S. State Department in conjunction with Muslim-majority governments (including Pakistan, Saudi Arabia, and Turkey), the United States is now ideally situated to create a long-term funding mechanism, or "global venture," that consolidates existing programs and seeds new initiatives. Done properly, within eight to ten years al-Qaeda's theology and ideology can become as unattractive among young Muslims as communism became to East Germans.

The Problem

Al-Qaeda and its ideological affiliates do not operate in a vacuum; rather, they feed off of ideas that have proliferated in Muslim communities over decades. A combination of religious literalism and conspiracist politics is at the core of their anti-Western ideology. These ideas include the beliefs that democracy is man-made and only extremist understandings of God's law should be enforced; that violent jihad is a Muslim obligation until "God's law" is manifest; that those who die pursuing it, including suicide bombers, are martyrs; and that the greatest obstacle to Islam's dominance is the modern West, led by the United States. Killing Americans, therefore, weakens an enemy that oppresses Muslims. Unless such ideas are challenged and discredited, extremist groups will continue to regenerate no matter how many terrorists are killed.

Developing Alternative Narratives

Organizations in the Middle East, Pakistan, and elsewhere are leading the way in advocating counternarratives to extremist messaging. Organizations like Khudi, a Pakistan-based campus network, use Muslim history to argue against radicals who twist the meaning of the word *umma* into a "nation united against infidels" (its correct, historical meaning is "community"). The Radical Middle Way, a Muslim organization based in London, holds public "question time" events with clerics from Egypt's prestigious al-Azhar seminary who use scripture to undermine the belief that suicide bombers are martyrs and to support democracy within an Islamic framework. Activists in Saudi Arabia and Egypt are using social media to challenge conspiracy theories and a pervasive sense of victimhood vis-à-vis the West. They work in hubs of extremist recruitment—mosques, community centers, universities, prisons, and websites—and target vulnerable youth with innovative programming.

Building on these and like-minded organizations and activists, CVE efforts must focus on:

- Educating Muslim thought leaders in mosques and on university campuses through workshops and testimonies from former radicals about why Islamist hard-liners threaten Muslim communities. In 2009, al-Qaeda and its affiliates killed more Muslims than non-Muslims. Muslims need to reclaim their faith because Islamist extremism endangers the very fabric of mainstream, moderate Islam.

- Providing financial support to moderates for establishing alternative satellite television channels across the Middle East. A region with bulging youth populations, high unemployment, low rates of reading books, and mass popularity of satellite television means radical clerics often provide unchallenged guidance on questions of religion and politics.
- Supporting the publication and dissemination of reading materials on normative Islam. Those looking for religious literature in the Middle East are often exposed to glossy publications from Gulf countries that promote a literalist, radical reading of Islam. Alternative and mainstream material exists in Egypt, Turkey, and Pakistan, but requires translation and targeted distribution on campuses, in bookshops, and in mosques.
- Initiating the around-the-clock presence of a professional, well-informed network of web-savvy Muslims who are active in Arab and Muslim chat rooms and on social media, refuting al-Qaeda propaganda with factual and scriptural arguments. The purpose is not to dissuade jihadis (that would be a bonus), but to ensure virtual audiences do not assume that extreme narratives are unchallenged and hence preponderant.
- Puncturing the popular perception that the United States is at war with Islam and Muslims by inviting religious leaders annually as guests of the U.S. Congress during the president's state of the union address. This respectful, high-visibility presence would generate Arab and Muslim media coverage that further dents anti-Americanism.

Pioneering a Global Venture

A cornerstone of the Obama administration's counterterrorism and CVE strategy is the Global Counterterrorism Forum. Launched in 2011, this effort has rightly identified the need for governments and experts to coordinate and share effective CVE strategies. The forum has inspired the creation of the Center of

Excellence for Countering Violent Extremism in Abu Dhabi, an institution focusing on training, research, and dialogue between nongovernmental organizations (NGOs) and governments that counter extremism. Building on these efforts by establishing a CVE global fund is a natural next step for the GCTF.

A global venture that identifies and funds counterradicalization projects in strategically important countries would be a first step in reversing the grip of the al-Qaeda narrative. Worthy efforts have been undertaken in the past, such as the State Department's public diplomacy initiatives and the appointment of a U.S. special representative to Muslim communities, but they have come up short by failing to address the ongoing funding crisis among anti-extremism organizations. A global venture, however, would build on existing efforts and financially strengthen Muslim civil society against extremism. The money to seed this project should come from a wide variety of individuals, organizations, and governments that share an interest in countering extremism. Public and private funding is readily available in Turkey and Gulf countries, from Muslim American communities, and from Western development and philanthropic organizations. Rooting this venture in a diverse network of partners would bolster the program's appeal while heading off the al-Qaeda allegation that it is an American plot.

Garnering support to combat radicalism under the umbrella of a global venture will require a centralized effort from a body that can lend the venture prestige, direction, and continuity. Based on existing American and Turkish cooperation at the GCTF, the United States should encourage Turkey to take the lead in establishing the global venture (the two currently lead the coordinating committee).

A Global Venture in Practice

Initially, the GCTF should convene an international conference of high-profile Muslim and non-Muslim philanthropists, imams, thinkers, community leaders, and government officials to define objectives and elect an oversight board from within their ranks.

They may wish to name the fund after a prominent Muslim historical figure to make it appeal to religious activists. Washington should encourage American philanthropies to advise the GCTF board on how to raise money and staff the venture.

The venture should be headquartered in Istanbul or a Gulf capital, locating it centrally in terms of both physical and religious geography. Based on interest levels from potential donors, funding levels for analogous ventures in the past, and absorptive capacity of future grantees, the global fund would require at least $300 million and a ten-year commitment by major donors at the outset to ensure the venture is sustainable and deeply rooted. Private and/or government-funded organizations could apply for grants of various sizes depending on the scope and activities of their proposed projects. With support, these organizations could organize youth camps, create social network–based websites to educate youth, provide speaking platforms for moderate imams, disseminate publications on Muslim campuses, offer scholarship opportunities, and create exchange programs for students to learn firsthand about Western government and society.

To ensure funds reach the right people, applicant organizations would need to demonstrate a commitment to religious pluralism, human rights, democracy, and nonviolence. Project proposals would require letters of support from groups credibly doing similar work on the ground or GCTF founding-member governments. Monitoring and evaluation would be central to the venture's mission, and therefore a robust staff will be needed to work with experts assigned to measure the success of funded programs and determine their eligibility for future funding. Existing philanthropies could be enlisted to advise on best practices.

Through sustained funding of existing efforts and supporting new initiatives in mosques, on campuses and satellite television, and through publications and online media, a global venture can target audiences through multiple avenues, maximizing efforts to discredit radical narratives.

> *"When a government official refused the 'lucrative offers,' threats against their personal safety and family soon followed."*

The Media Has Been Complicit in the Rise of ISIS and Other Extremist Groups

Bouthania Shaaban

In the following excerpted viewpoint, Bouthania Shaaban discusses the efforts made to destabilize and delegitimize the government in Syria and how the country was then perceived to be a so-called breeding ground for extremist groups, such as ISIS. Shaaban, a Syrian politician and adviser to Syrian president Bashar al-Assad, details how members of the Syrian government at all levels were invited, or even pressured, to "defect" in favor of the Western and regional coalition looking to out Assad's regime. Shaaban cites personal experience and Western media sources to show both sides of her argument and how Western interference gave rise to these new extremist groups attempting to gain control of countries in the Middle East. Shaaban is political and media advisor to the Syrian presidency and was nominated for a Nobel Peace Prize in 2005.

As you read, consider the following questions:

1. How does the author describe the Syrian government's immediate response to the protests?
2. What was the "Geneva Communiqué"?
3. How did Russia support Syria in a way the United States failed to do?

This essay examines the role of Western and regional players (i.e. Turkey, Saudi Arabia, and Qatar) in inflaming the conflict and the growth of terrorism in Syria. It examines the attempts to break up Syria's civilian and military institutions, the delegitimization of the Syrian government, the attempts to procure a UN mandate for a military intervention in Syria, the imposition of suffocating economic sanctions on Syria, and most importantly the support that Western and regional powers gave to a plethora of armed groups, including al-Qaeda and ISIS, to fight the Syrian government. The latter point is scrutinized in order to highlight how the United States, and its allies in the region, cynically employed extremist groups in Syria to achieve geopolitical gains, thus leading to wider regional upheaval, the effects of which will most certainly go beyond the West Asia region.

This essay then moves to examine the crucial differences between the US-led campaign against ISIS, and the Russian efforts in Syria, in addition to examining the central role of the Syrian government and army in the fight against terrorism. Finally, this paper examines the dangers of extremist ideologies being espoused and promoted by governments and individuals in the Gulf region, and their effect on social cohesion in targeted countries, with Syria being the latest example. Throughout the proceeding points, special attention will be given to the role played by Western and Gulf mass media and the false narratives it propagated about the conflict in Syria and the wider West Asia region.

A Prelude to ISIS: Western destabilization of Syria

The Syrian government's immediate response to the protests, despite the violent incidents at the very onset of events, was reconciliatory, as some of the demonstrators had genuine demands. On 24 March 2011, the Syrian leadership convened a long and important meeting in an effort to contain what seemed to be a looming crisis. I was asked to hold a press conference in order to acknowledge, in the name of the leadership, the people's legitimate demands and to announce decisions and measures that addressed most of these demands.

On that day, I announced to the Syrian people the lifting of emergency laws, in place since 1963, and a comprehensive reform package that would lead to further political freedoms, a multi-party law, and the drafting of a new constitution for Syria. Next day, people told me that they out to have dinner celebrating Syria averting a looming crisis. A feeling of relief prevailed all over the country due to the leadership's quick response to the demands.

President Bashar al-Assad also ordered the immediate release of all those detained during the unfortunate events that took place in Deraa the week before. Thousands of Syrians from all walks of life, dozens of delegations from all Syrian cities and villages flocked to the Presidential Palace for direct dialogue with the President. I also met many delegations, including local opposition. I was most happy to engage the youth, connect with their ideas, and listen to their aspirations; the mood was far from confrontational. Many more dialogue initiatives were taken at every level of government and civil society.

This conciliatory approach, however, was met with much worse intransigence by those who claimed to represent the Syrian people and was by then occupying much of the airtime on Al-Jazeera and al-Arabyia. These two channels played an inciting role, encouraging people to protest and rebel against the Syrian government, and they constituted the primary source for news about Syria to all Western media outlets.

On 29 July 2011, an obscure group of seven men, dressed in military uniforms announced the formation of the "Free Syrian Army" on YouTube. The world was supposed to believe that out of 300,000 officers and soldiers constituting the Syrian Armed Forces, seven men were to represent a legitimate fighting force to replace that institution. Apparently, they did, at least to the West and their Turkish and Arab backers. The venture grew into 15,000-armed men based at camps in southern Turkey. Their spokesperson promised immanent action to "liberate" Syria.[1] Turkey, a member of NATO, was now hosting an army of insurgents on its territory, the composition of which was largely unknown, threatening to invade a sovereign nation with the aim of overthrowing its government under the veneer of "freedom fighters."

The depth of Turkey's commitment to sponsor these terrorists, whether in 2011, or later in 2015 when they became known as ISIS and al-Nusra, is represented by the shooting down of the Russian fighter jet operating against terrorists in Syria.

Only five years later that Western think tanks woke up to the fact that "neither desertions nor defections have significantly weakened the [Syrian] military or its chain of command."[2] A study by the Carnegie Endowment's Middle East Center found that most "defections", little as they may be, happened for economic motives and were mainly towards "well-funded jihadist militias," as opposed to the so-called Free Syrian Army.[3]

The attempt to break up Syria's institutions was not limited to the armed forces. Many officials, from all levels of government, including myself, were invited, and in many ways pressured and harassed, to "defect." They were offered financial incentives and —ironically—a place in the government of "new Syria." When a government official refused the "lucrative offers," threats against their personal safety and family soon followed. Eventually, many Syrian government officials and I were sanctioned by the European Union and the United States, simply for refusing to quit our job and relinquish our duty. The objective of breaking up both the military and the civilian institutions of Syria by any means necessary were clear from the onset.

On 18 August 2011, US President Barack Obama called for the ouster of President Asad.[4] The United States was yet again committing itself to changing the political regime of a sovereign country. Obama's statement constituted a green light for another serious attempt to usurp legitimacy from the Syrian government. By the end of August a group of "opposition" figures gathered in Istanbul, under the auspices of the Turkish government, announced the formation of the "Syrian National Council." This grouping enjoyed no popular or political legitimacy, yet Western nations, Turkey, as well as Qatar and Saudi Arabia began to deal with them as the sole representative of the Syrian people, aiding and abating their intransigence and their refusal to any national dialogue initiatives that would end the crisis and the bloodshed.

We cannot ascertain what sort of deals was made under the table—similar to those between the French intelligence services and the Libyan National Transitional Council. The efforts were given a serious impetus when in November 2011, Qatar and Saudi Arabia, backed by the nascent Muslim-Brotherhood-led regimes in Egypt, Tunisia and Libya, succeeded in freezing Syria's membership in the Arab League. The decision was followed by Arab sanctions against Syria, setting the stage for American and European enforced single measure sanctions that would prevent Syrians from acquiring many essentials including heating fuel and cancer treatments.[5]

The anti-Syria efforts culminated in the ironically-named "Friends of Syria Group" meeting in Tunisia in February 2012, which included among others the United States, France, UK, and Germany, in addition to Turkey, Qatar, Saudi Arabia and other Arab countries. This group tried to confer legitimacy and offer support to the so-called National Council and Free Syrian Army; calling for action-a-la-Libya that would see them replace the legitimate Syrian government.[6] The "activists" on the ground linked to the Turkey-based opposition began to circulate banners calling for a no-fly zone, a buffer zone, and international "humanitarian" intervention in Syria.[7]

These demonstrators were filmed and Western and Gulf-Arab mainstream media showed the clips repeatedly; while footage showing hundreds of thousands flooding the streets of Damascus and other cities supporting their government against any foreign intervention did not make the cut.

Challenging Western Hegemony: The Double Veto

The "Friends of Syria" sought tirelessly to gain a UN mandate for the process of delegitimizing the Syrian government, and imposing the Turkey-based "National Council" as a representative of the Syrian people; let alone soliciting a mandate to carry on a military intervention similar to the one in Libya. These efforts to breach Syria's sovereignty were repeatedly met by a joint Russian-Chinese veto at the United Nations Security Council (four in total by May 2014). The first attempt was on 4 October 2011, followed by a second one in February 2012. In the night before the second attempt was made under Chapter Seven of the UN Charter, violent clashes erupted in the central city of Homs. Media outlets reported throughout the night that Syrian security forces were committing atrocities and killing hundreds of people, just hours before the Security Council session. This behavior became a pattern. On 19 July 2012, the Security Council met to discuss another Syria-related resolution presented by the Western powers, and it was again blocked by a Russian-Chinese double veto.

Just three days before this session, four of Syria's top generals were assassinated, and thousands of gunmen tried to break into the city centers of Aleppo and Damascus, in an operation they dubbed "The Volcano." Information leaked two years after the event indicated that this was a complicated American-Turkish plan to overtake Damascus. Russia's foreign minister Sergey Lavrov explained the reasoning behind the double veto(s): "The veto [right] is not a privilege but a great responsibility. Thanks to the veto imposed by Russia and China several times we can say that a chance for transition to the political settlement process has emerged in the Syrian crisis. And it is absolutely true that the Russia-China veto has prevented Syria's transformation into Libya.[8]"

Outside the Security Council, an international working group, which in addition to the Arab League, France, Britain, and the United States, included Russia and China, met in Geneva in June 2012. The group issued the "Geneva Communiqué," which emphasized a Syria-led political solution for the crisis based on dialogue between Syrians. Western powers however largely ignored the outcomes of the meeting when they began to recognize the Syrian National Coalition (the offspring of the National Council) as the sole legitimate representative of the Syrian people.

The Arab League, under Qatari leadership, went as far as giving them Syria's seat at the 2013 Arab Summit in Doha. This unelected "coalition," like its predecessor, enjoyed no legitimate popular mandate, little presence on the ground in Syria, and many of its members had ties to terrorist organizations. Conferring legitimacy on this group of Istanbul-based figures enabled them to call on Western and Arab countries to fund and arm the so-called Free Syrian Army. This "army" however proved to be no more than a franchise name; arms and funding actually went to the real forces on the ground, i.e. the radical Islamist terrorist groups –as the following section of this paper will show.

The dismantling of Syria's chemical stockpiles in late 2013 was supposed to be the first joint action between Russia and the United States that may lead to a political solution of the Syrian crisis. It was in this spirit that both the US and Russia called for convening *Geneva II Conference* in Monteux, and then in Geneva in January and February of 2014. Although Sergey Lavrov and John Kerry agreed to conciliatory opening speeches, Kerry's speech may, in all fairness, be described as a war speech against the Syrian government.

Two important things preceded the speech. First, the US total rejection of Iran's presence, despite the fact that the UN General Secretary had already sent an invitation to Iran but was later forced to rescind it. Second, the United States and Turkey rejected the presence of any Syrian opposition except the Turkey-based "Syrian National Coalition." In the two rounds of talks in January and February 2014, representative of the Syrian government stressed that the top priority in Syria was the fight against terrorism, and that all countries should participate in this effort because terrorism in Syria constituted a real threat for the region and the world at large. No one was prepared to heed the warnings of the Syrian government or to take the dangers to world peace seriously.

The West joins forces with al-Qaeda

It only took fourteen years after the tragic events of 9/11 for a representative of a Jihadi group closely linked to al-Qaeda to be able to write an op-ed for a major American publication: *the Washington Post*. Labib Nahhas, the head of foreign relations for Ahrar al-Sham group, wrote an article calling on the United States to join efforts with his organization to "end the reign" of Bashar al-Asad.[9] Ahrar al-Sham is, of course, a terrorist organization that adopts Salafi-Jihadism as its ideology and is part of the Jaysh al-Fatah (Army of Conquest) coalition, which also includes Jabhat al-Nusra, the official al-Qaeda branch in Syria. Al-Qaeda had taken advantage of the chaos in Syria, as it did in Iraq and Libya, to appear on the scene first as al-Nusra, later joined by the so-called Islamic State of Iraq and Syria (formerly al-Qaeda in Iraq). Yet when the Syrian government first warned of al-Qaeda's presence in Syria, the declaration was met with doubts, and at times ridicule, from mass media.

Although Syria had suffered terrorist attacks in the decade before. When al-Nusra claimed responsibility for a dual car bombing in Damascus on 23 December 2011, the Istanbul-based opposition accused the Syrian government of fabricating the whole episode.

Al-Qaeda in Syria, in both its al-Nusra and ISIS manifestations, is however very real, as the world was soon to find out. In fact, so real was al-the Qaeda threat in Syria that the US would come to create a wobbly coalition, whose simple purpose is exterminating ISIS. After 9/11, the Syrians sympathized with the US, saying: "We know how you feel, we have been there before in the 1980s, when terrorism struck in the heart of our towns and cities." We actually shared intelligence with them and were thanked by the Bush Administration for helping save American lives during a 2006 terrorist on the American Embassy in Damascus.[10] We expected the same from Americans—both people and government—but instead, we got nothing but a vicious media campaign and US backing for an ugly sectarian war.

When violence escalated in Syria, the "Free Syrian Army" franchise quickly disappeared from the battlefield, but not from the media. The real forces on the ground were al-Nusra, Jaysh al-Islam (Army of Islam), Ahrar al-Sham, Jaysh al- Mujahedeen (Army of Mujahedeen) and other Jihadi groups –including ISIS. These groups, with foreign support, soon turned major city such as Aleppo and Homs into battlefields, barricading themselves in residential areas and causing a mass-exodus of civilians.

The Syrian Army was soon fighting on an endless number of fronts. It had to protect neighborhoods and towns, power lines and water sources, factories and public institutions. Everything and everyone was under attack, as this chapter will show in a later section. Jihadis from dozens of countries, including veteran Chechen ones, soon joined the terrorists in Syria.[11] NATO weapons were smuggled from wartorn Libya to Syrian jihadis.[12] Terror tactics never seen before were used against the Syrian people. Terrorists would dig tunnels underneath residential areas, fill them with explosives, and then detonate them, knocking down entire buildings. They would relentlessly shell city centers with mortars, rockets and "hell cannons"—a nightmarish weapon that lobs canisters loaded with hundreds of pounds of explosives and shrapnel.

It wasn't late before ISIS (the Islamic State of Iraq and Syria) began to dominate the scene. Yet when the organization scored its first big "victory" in the summer of 2013, overrunning the Menagh airbase north of Aleppo with its ally al-Nusra, after dozens of suicide attacks, the Istanbul-based opposition issued a statement congratulating the Syrian people for this "achievement.[13]" Al-Jazeera interviewed ISIS's war chief Omar al-Shishani (the Chechen) from within the airbase, a man who would mastermind the organization's biggest atrocities from beheadings to the Mount Sinjar tragedy. The reader might notice a discrepancy here; I am mostly citing Western media sources, yet at the same time criticizing them. The reason is quite simple. Even though the world media reported the Jihadi surge, the dominant narrative was that all of it was in response to Syrian government atrocities, claiming that the "regime" had purposely transformed the country into a magnet for terrorists.

This narrative remained in place even when ISIS became the West's "number one enemy" in the region, in addition to its sidekick al-Nusra. However, no one was asking the real and necessary question: How were all these Jihadis able to group in the tens of thousands, arm and fund themselves and cross into Syria? Regardless of what was being presented to the world, decision makers in the West, and especially the United States, not only knew very well the factors behind the escalation of the conflict in Syria, but also helped them grow. The weapon shipments from Libya mentioned above, were actually funneled through a CIA and MI6-run back channel highway dubbed the "rat line."[14] These weapons crossed from southern Turkey into Syria to the hands of the Jihadis, al-Nusra and ISIS.[15] Furthermore, Western powers knew exactly the eventual outcome of these actions. A recently declassified secret US intelligence report, written in August 2012, predicted—and even welcomed—the prospect of a "Salafist principality" in eastern Syria and an al-Qaeda-controlled Islamic state in Syria and Iraq.[16] The American Defense Intelligence Agency document identifies al-Qaeda in Iraq (which morphed into ISIS) and fellow Jihadi groups as the "major forces driving the insurgency in Syria," and states that "western countries, the Gulf states and Turkey" were supporting the opposition's efforts to take control of Eastern Syria.[17] Raising the "possibility of establishing a declared or undeclared Salafist principality," the Pentagon report goes on, "this is exactly what the supporting powers to the opposition want, in order to isolate the Syrian regime, which is considered the strategic depth of the Shia expansion (Iraq and Iran)."[18] Last year, US Vice President Joe Biden complained to students at the Harvard Kennedy School that America's biggest problem was its allies. "The Turks, the Saudis, the Emirates, etc., what were they doing? They were so determined to take down [President Bashar] al-Asad and essentially have a proxy Sunni-Shia war, what did they do? They poured hundreds of millions of dollars and tens, thousands of tons of weapons into anyone who would fight against Asad."[19] He also said that Turkey admitted it had let too many foreign fighters cross its border into Syria. These policies ended up helping militants linked to al-Qaeda (i.e. al-Nusra Front) and ultimately ISIS, Biden explained.[20] Biden eventually apologized for making these remarks, which came weeks after the United Nations Security Council adopted a set of resolutions barring countries and individuals from funding and arming both ISIS and al-Nusra. Nevertheless, these resolutions were never truly implemented as no action has been taken against countries or individuals known to be financing, arming or facilitating movements of terrorists.

The United States blacklisted al-Nusra Front in 2012, and bombed its headquarters in 2014. Nonetheless, by early 2015, America and its allies were preparing another strike against the Syrian government, the spearhead of which was none other than al-Qaeda's Nusra Front. In the spring of 2015, Saudi Arabia, Turkey and Qatar put together a nightmarish amalgamation of Jihadi groups to strike in northern Syria. "The Army of Conquest" coalition included in addition to Ahrar al- Sham and al-Nusra Front, groups of Central Asian, Chechen and Chinese-Uyghur Jihadis.[21] Advancing from their bases in southern Turkey, the terrorist hoard stormed the Syrian province of Idleb. Outrageously, the US-run Military Operations Center (Also known as *the MOC*), based in the Turkish city of Antioch, planned the offensive.[22] Furthermore, the United States supplied some groups it deemed "moderate" with US-made TOW anti-tank missiles to help with the Idleb offensive.[23]

Yellow Journalism

The Spanish-American War is often referred to as the first "media war." During the 1890s, journalism that sensationalized—and sometimes even manufactured—dramatic events was a powerful force that helped propel the United States into war with Spain. Led by newspaper owners William Randolph Hearst and Joseph Pulitzer, journalism of the 1890s used melodrama, romance, and hyperbole to sell millions of newspapers—a style that became known as yellow journalism.

The term yellow journalism came from a popular *New York World* comic called "Hogan's Alley," which featured a yellow-dressed character named the "the yellow kid." Determined to compete with Pulitzer's World in every way, rival *New York Journal* owner William Randolph Hearst copied Pulitzer's sensationalist style. In response, Pulitzer commissioned another cartoonist to create a second yellow kid. Soon, the sensationalist press of the 1890s became a competition, and the journalistic style was coined "yellow journalism."

Yellow journals like the *New York Journal* and the *New York World* relied on sensationalist headlines to sell newspapers. William Randolph Hearst understood that a war with Cuba would not only sell his papers, but also move him into a position of national prominence. From Cuba, Hearst's star reporters wrote stories designed to tug at the heartstrings of Americans. Horrific tales described the situation in Cuba—female prisoners, executions, valiant rebels fighting, and starving women and children figured in many of the stories that filled the newspapers. But it was the sinking of the battleship *Maine* in Havana Harbor that gave Hearst his big story—war. After the sinking of the *Maine*, the Hearst newspapers, with no evidence, unequivocally blamed the Spanish, and soon U.S. public opinion demanded intervention.

Today, historians point to the Spanish-American War as the first press-driven war. Although it may be an exaggeration to claim that Hearst and the other yellow journalists started the war, it is fair to say that the press fueled the public's passion for war. Without sensational headlines and stories about Cuban affairs, the mood for Cuban intervention may have been very different. At the dawn of the twentieth century, the United States emerged as a world power, and the U.S. press proved its influence.

"Yellow Journalism," Great Projects Film Company, Inc.

These missiles were launched at the Syrian Army's tanks and vehicles, clearing the way for the Jihadi Army to overrun the cities of Idleb, Ariha, and Jisr al-Shughur, killing and displacing thousands of innocent civilians—many of whom eventually found their way to Europe across the Mediterranean.

Comparing Russian and American Efforts Against terrorism

In August 2014, the United States and a coalition of 60 countries (including Saudi Arabia and Qatar), decided it was time to "degrade" and eventually destroy ISIS. Dr. Frankenstein was coming after one of the monsters he created; except in reality, he was not. The supposed US-led military campaign against the so-called Islamic State is, for all intents and purposes, a phony war. In a year of airstrikes, the US-led coalition conducted an average of some 15 airstrikes per day against an organization controlling a territory the size of Great Britain.[24]

To put this number into perspective, during Operation Desert Strom in 1991, the United States launched 1000 airstrikes a day against Iraq. During the 2003 invasion of Iraq, the American Air Force carried some 700 airstrikes a day. The air campaign against ISIS, which Obama promised would help eventually destroy the organization, was little more than a slap on the wrist. Consequently, in a year of American airstrikes, the terrorist group was able to increase the area it controls, conquering the Iraqi city of Ramadi (capital of Anbar province) and the ancient Syrian city of Palmyra. ISIS was so at ease in its areas of control that it began to mint coins, establish schools, and carry out a systematic destruction of ancient ruins in both Iraq and Syria. World heritage sites in Palmyra, Nimrod and Nineveh were razed; American satellites captured images of the destruction, but apparently failed to notice those who placed the bombs.

Looking for foot soldiers in Syria to join its campaign, the US opted to arm "moderate" Syrian opposition group for the purpose of fighting ISIS. For the Idleb offensive against the Syrian government, the United States and its allies were able to group and equip 50,000 fighters (mostly Jihadis), but when it came to fighting terrorism, the US training program drew in a whopping 50 "moderates." The fifty men enjoyed a lavish training program paid for with half a billion dollars of American taxpayers' money. But when they entered Syria, al-Qaeda's Nusra front took away their American-supplied weapons and threw them in prison.[25] The US eventually cancelled the program, but the farce did not end there.[26] The Obama administration decided to airdrop 50 tons of weapons directly into the hands of the "moderates," now calling themselves the "Syrian Democratic Forces." [27] How many shipments would follow and in whose hands they would end up? No one knows.

If the United States and its allies are not out to destroy ISIS, what is their real objective then? I would not like to delve into much speculation, but one cannot ignore facts on the ground. Since the US-led collation began its campaign, ISIS has expanded. The terrorist group is attracting more foreign recruits, as the Turkish border with Syria remains wide open. In Mount Sinjar in Iraq, the United States did not allow Kurdish Peshmerga forces, in control of commanding heights, to target the road liking ISIS-controlled cities of Mosul and Raqqah. On 12 November 2015, the United States reversed its decision and in one day the Kurdish Peshmerga replaced ISIS in the Sinjar province. But where did the men of ISIS go? My conjuncture is that they shaved their beards and changed their uniforms, and joined the so-called "Syrian Democratic Forces" which the US has created not to fight ISIS, but in order to fight the Syrian Army and help the Kurds to establish an autonomous entity in the north of Syria as a prelude to partitioning the country, as they are also trying to partition Iraq.

Other terrorist groups such as al-Nusra and Jaysh al-Fatah also continue to expand, with support from the US and its allies. Is this failure the result of flawed policies? Does the United States and its allies badly misunderstand the region? Or is there a deliberate course of action to achieve certain geopolitical gains, and perhaps redraw the maps of both Iraq and Syria? In either case, the Syrian people and their government are the ones facing the mortal threat of the so-called Islamic State and the host of other terror organization. While American and other Western decision-makers could afford the luxury of trial and error from the comfort of their offices halfway around the earth, Syrians have paid a high price in both their blood and their livelihood standing up courageously against global terrorism. Decisive action should have been taken, if anybody wanted a way out for Syria, but it was not by the west.

In his speech before the 70th session of the UN General Assembly in September 2015, Russia's President Vladimir Putin criticized the export of the so-called 'democratic' revolutions, which unleashed poverty and violence instead of the triumph of democracy, especially in the Middle East. He cited the examples of Iraq and Libya, where the Untied States changed political regimes by force in defiance of international laws and norms creating power vacuums, which in turn led to the emergence of lawless areas that immediately started to be filled with extremists and terrorists. "We think it is an enormous mistake to refuse to cooperate with the Syrian government and its armed forces who are valiantly fighting terrorism face to face…we should finally acknowledge that no one but President Assad's armed forces and Kurdish militia are truly fighting Islamic State and other terrorist organizations in Syria," said Putin. The Russian President then proposed the joining of efforts and the creation of a broad international coalition against terrorism. He also proposed discussions at the UN Security Council about a resolution aimed at coordinating forces to confront ISIS and other terrorist organizations, based on the principles of the UN Charter.

Putin's speech reflected Russia's ample understanding of the situation in Syria since 2011, which stems largely from the continuous strategic dialogue between Damascus and Moscow. This dialogue goes back decades, and has intensified dramatically during the Syrian crisis. Since 2014, Russia has been providing technical military assistance to Iraq, Syria and other states in the region, with the goal of combating extremism and ISIS. Politically, Russia has worked tirelessly to establish a broad regional and international coalition against terrorism, months before Putin's speech at the UN. Upon meeting President Putin in Moscow in June 2015, Syria's foreign minister Mr. Walid Moualem and myself welcomed Russia's efforts in trying to establish such a coalition. However, Syria seriously doubted that the United States and its allies, especially Turkey and Saudi Arabia would be forthcoming. Our estimate was accurate; the United States and its allies responded negatively to all initiatives, leaving Russia no alternative but to act decisively against the terrorist threat endangering Syria, the West Asia region and Russia itself, if not the entire world.

So, on 30 September, upon a request from the Syrian government, the Russian air force began conducting airstrikes against the different terrorist groups operating on Syrian soil. At the moment of writing, the strikes are ongoing, coupled with a massive ground offensive by the Syrian Army on many fronts to weed out the terrorists and liberate Syrian cities and villages.

The performance of the Russians in Syria has embarrassed the United States. The Russians presented the Americans with satellite pictures showing ISIS terrorists moving for miles on the roads to Palmyra, while US satellites observed, with no action whatsoever taken against them by the American-led coalition.

The Russians also presented the United States with other satellite pictures showing ISIS terrorists moving oil from north of Syria to Sinjar in Iraq where the oil is sold through Iraqi Kurdistan in exchange for weapons and ammunition that go back to Syria. All this happens along a road in the midst of a desert, which makes them an easy target for American airstrikes had there been a will to do that. On the other hand, after only two months into the Russian airstrikes in Syria, the Syrian Army had been enabled to liberate large areas from ISIS and al-Nusra Front. As a result the Russians are gaining credibility in Syria and the Arab World at large, while the Americans and the West no longer enjoy the trust of the Arab people.

Conclusion: Syria, a Gateway to Asia

By deliberately supporting terrorists in Syria under the banner of changing the regime (which is against international laws), Western countries have aided Turkey, Saudi Arabia and Qatar in what in reality is an all-out war against Syria in an effort to destroy the country and eliminate the role it has been playing in the region and the world since time immemorial. Syria today is a Gordian knot, and its unraveling threatens the whole of Asia. As this paper has tried to show, what happened in Syria was a grand geopolitical game under the guise of a movement for democracy (i.e. the Arab Spring). Little attention is paid to Libya nowadays; the country has sunk into chaos even though NATO intervened less than a fortnight after the "armed rebellion" began.

Today, ISIS is devouring Libya piece by piece, and Sarkozy's and Cameron's promise to build a democracy there proved to be hollow. The use of religious fanaticism, media complacency, and terrorist groups to overthrow the legitimate government of Syria in order to achieve geopolitical gains is an operational model that might very well repeated anywhere else. The West, Saudi Arabia, and Turkey are the main culprits. Russia, China, Iran, and the BRICS have stood up to this attempt in various forms; starting with the double veto up to the Russian campaign against terrorism in Syria. Yet the Syrian model could be repeated anywhere in Asia, whenever Western interests might find it useful. Beyond geopolitical machinations, India and other Asian countries should pay heed to the poisonous ideologies espoused by Gulf countries. Wahhabi penetration of diverse societies, sowing hatred and extremism is enabled by their vast wealth; hydrocarbon sources today are their main funder of terrorism in the world. India and China should be more involved in West Asia, not only to secure energy sources, but to make sure that those sources do not became a weapon to destroy Asian societies from within through extremism and terrorism.

Notes

1 Ruth Sherlock, '15,000 strong' army gathers to take on Syria', *The Telegraph*, 3 November 2011.

2 Dorothy Ohl, Holger Albrecht, Kevin Koehler, 'For Money or Liberty? The Political Economy of Military Desertion and Rebel Recruitment in the Syrian Civil War,' Carnegie Middle East Center, 24 November 2015.

3 Ibid.

4 Scott Wilson, 'Assad must go, Obama says', *The Washington Post*, 18 August 2011.

5 Neil MacFarquhar and Nada Bakri, 'Isolating Syria, Arab League Imposes Broad Sanctions', *The New York Times*, 27 November 2011.

6 Arshad Mohammed and Christian Lowe, 'Friends of Syria condemn Assad but see more killing', *Reuters*, 24 February 2012.

7 'Annan renews call for UN unity on Syria', Al-Jazeera, 16 March 2012.

8 'Chance to begin political settlement process in Syria exists – Lavrov', Russia Beyond the Headlines, 20 April 2015.

9 Labib al-Nahhas, 'The deadly consequences of mislabeling Syria's revolutionaries', *The Washington Post*, 10 July 2015.

10 CNN, 'U.S. lauds Syrian forces in embassy attack, 12 September 2006.

11 Thomas Grove and Mariam Karouny, 'Syria War: Rebels Joined By Chechnya Islamic Militants In 'Jihad' Against Assad', The Huffington Post, 3 June 2013.

12 C. J. Chivers, Eric Schmitt and Mark Mazzetti, 'In Turnabout, Syria Rebels Get Libyan Weapons', *The New York Times*, 21 June 2013.

13 Nour Malas and Rima Abushakra, 'Islamists Seize Airbase Near Aleppo', *The Wall Street Journal*, 6 August 2013.

14 Seymour M. Hersh, 'The Red Line and the Rat Line', *The London Review of Books*, 17 April 2014.

15 Ibid.

16 Seumas Milne, 'Now the truth emerges: how the US fueled the rise of Isis in Syria and Iraq', *The Guardian*, 3 June 2015.

17 Ibid.

18 Ibid.

19 Barbara Plett Usher, 'Joe Biden apologized over IS remarks, but was he right?', *The BBC*, 7 October 2014.

20 Ibid.

21 Caleb Weiss, 'Turkistan Islamic Party in Syria involved in new Idlib offensive', *Long Wars Journal*, 23 April 2015.

22 Charles Lister, 'Why Assad is Losing', *Foreign Policy Magazine*, 5 May 2015.

23 Ibid.

24 'Special Report: Operation Inherent Resolve', *The United States Department of Defense*, 6 October 2015.

25 'U.S.-trained Syrian rebels gave equipment to Nusra: U.S. military', Reuters, 26 September 2015.

26 Jim Milkaszewski, Erik Ortiz and Laura Saravia, 'Pentagon Ends Program to Train Syrian Rebels, Starts Revamped Initiative', *MSNBC*, 9 October 2015.

27 Barbara Starr, 'U.S. delivers 50 tons of ammunition to Syria rebel groups', *CNN*, 12 October 2015.

> *"Strikingly, over half of under-35s in Japan say they are more interested in soft news topics than hard news."*

When It Comes to News, What Sells Matters

Reuters Institute for the Study of Journalism

In the following viewpoint, writers from the Reuters Institute for the Study of Journalism discuss recent trends in the popularity of "hard" and "soft" news. "Hard" news is considered to be timely reports, such as politics, international affairs, and business news, while "soft" news includes entertainment, celebrity, and lifestyle topics. On the international stage, "hard" news topics like politics tend to be more popular in countries such as Germany, Turkey, and the United States, while the Japanese tend to be more interested in topics like celebrity news. Additionally, the authors of the report note a significant difference in preference along gender lines. Reuters Institute for the Study of Journalism is an international research center in the comparative study of journalism affiliated with the University of Oxford.

As you read, consider the following questions:

1. What is the difference between "hard" and "soft" news?
2. What demographic is more likely to be interested in "soft" news according to the viewpoint?
3. What is the main source of news for those people interested in soft news?

This year we have collected more detailed data on the level of interest people have in different news topics across countries and between demographics. Political news is considered most important in Germany, Turkey, and the United States, partly no doubt due to the ongoing presidential election and the drama around Donald Trump's candidacy. International news is of particular interest in Germany and Austria as well as Ireland. Japanese are most interested in entertainment and celebrity news, with the Spanish, Danes, French, and Germans showing the least interest. Regional news is most important in Germany, Finland, and Spain, reflecting the relative importance of devolved political power in those countries and the media systems that have grown up around this.

But in addition to country-based differences we can see clear differences in gender, with men more interested in subjects like sport and politics and women paying more attention to stories about health and the environment. Again this plays into the debate over distributed content and may help explain why women are often less likely to directly access news websites dominated by politics and business.

Hard and Soft News

We can also divide consumers into groups based on their interest in 'hard' and 'soft' news topics. 'Hard' news is typically used to refer to topics that are usually timely, important and consequential, such as politics, international affairs and business news. Conversely, soft news topics include entertainment, celebrity, and lifestyle news.

We asked our survey respondents to rate their interest in several news topics on a five-point scale. We then used this data to compute average levels of interest in hard and soft news for each respondent. Subsequently we compared the scores for hard and soft news, and divided respondents into three groups; those who are more interested in hard news topics, those who are more interested in soft news, and those whose interest in both is the same.

On average, in every country we see that interest levels are higher for hard news topics. However, this is likely to be influenced by social desirability bias (the idea that it is more acceptable to interested in certain types of news) as well the norms of the traditional news agenda. At the individual level, people with a high degree of interest in hard news also tend to be the most interested in soft news, and vice versa.

Yet we still see a significant minority in every country that report they are more interested in soft news topics than hard news. The size of this group varies country by country. Around one-third in Japan (34%) and Korea (33%) say they are more interested in soft news. However, less than one in five say the same in most other countries. The preference for hard news is particularly strong in Greece (81%), Spain (77%), Denmark (77%), and Germany (76%).

If we focus on those that say they are more interested in soft news, we see that they are more likely to be young and female. In countries such as Japan and Italy, where interest in soft news is high, women are almost twice as likely as men to be more interested in soft news topics compared to hard.

In every country younger people are more likely to be more interested in soft news topics. Strikingly, over half of under-35s in Japan say they are more interested in soft news topics than hard news.

Of course, what people say they are interested in may not accurately reflect what they actually do. Nonetheless, we observe some differences in consumption among those that are more interested in soft news. Most noticeably, they are considerably more likely to say that social media is their main source of news.

Over one in five of those more interested in soft news in Spain (21%), Italy (20%), and the United States (26%) say that social media are their main source of news. This has a knock-on effect for related aspects of offsite news consumption, with people who prefer soft news more likely to watch news video on social media, and more likely to participate in news coverage. However, this is in part caused by the fact that younger people in general are more likely to use social media for news.

Periodical and Internet Sources Bibliography

The following articles have been selected to supplement the diverse views presented in this chapter.

Wajahat Ali, Eli Clifton, Matthew Duss, Lee Fang, Scott Keyes, and Faiz Shakir, "The Roots of the Islamophobia Network in America", Center for American Progress, August 26, 2011. https://www.americanprogress.org/issues/religion/reports/2011/08/26/10165/fear-inc/.

CBS News, "Advocates Fear Rise in Anti-Muslim Attacks after Paris, San Bernardino," CBS News, December 10, 2015. http://www.cbsnews.com/news/advocates-fear-rise-in-anti-muslim-attacks-after-paris-san-bernardino/.

Eszter Hargittai, W. Russell Neuman, and Olivia Curry, "Taming the Information Tide: Perceptions of Information Overload in the American Home," Information Society, May 23, 2011. http://www.tandfonline.com/doi/abs/10.1080/01972243.2012.669450.

Caitlin MacNeal, "The Stunningly Long List of Anti-Muslim Hate Crimes Since San Bernardino," Talking Points Memo, December 15, 2015. http://talkingpointsmemo.com/news/anti-muslim-attacks-after-san-bernardino.

Domenico Montanaro, "6 Times Obama Called on Muslim Communities to Do More About Extremism", NPR, December 7, 2015. http://www.npr.org/2015/12/07/458797632/6-times-obama-called-on-muslim-communities-to-do-more-about-extremism.

Race Forward, "Moving the Race Conversation Forward," Race Forward Center for Racial Justice Innovation, January 22, 2014. https://www.raceforward.org/research/reports/moving-race-conversation-forward.

Alexandra Zavis, "Young Homegrown Extremists Pose Threat in Saudi Arabia," *Los Angeles Times*, May 31, 2015. http://www.latimes.com/world/middleeast/la-fg-saudi-islamic-state-20150531-story.html.

CHAPTER 3

How Does Technology Help Alternative Media?

Chapter Preface

I t is clear that modern technology benefits both the free press and the alternative media. The rapid rise in the number of social media users will continue to grow exponentially over the next few years, leading to constant changes in the way people communicate with one another. Social media is no longer something that is "nice to have," but a necessary component to all aspects of society, whether business or personal.

But while social media and other digital forms of communication continue this rapid growth, the laws governing them have come much slower because there is no clear consensus on how to govern the actions taken on the Internet. So, while the Internet makes it easy for marginalized groups to bring attention to their plight, especially in autocratic countries, there has been a trend in recent years where governments all around the world are attempting to crack down on civil unrest and stymie the spread of democracy. Human rights and the Internet are irrevocably linked, and actions must be taken to ensure free and open Internet access, especially to all citizens living in developing countries.

The expansion of new media in the Middle East showcases why alternative forms of media can be used to foster democratic change in the region. Abrupt regime changes like that of Hosni Mubarak's in Egypt show the benefits of peer-to-peer communication, though it is currently very expensive and difficult for many to access. Satellite broadcasting companies that cater directly to those living in the Middle East are paving the way for more media freedoms, though there are ethical questions considering who owns these companies, many of which are based in Europe and owned by people looking to peddle a specific agenda.

Conversely, this chapter delves more into the issues surrounding Internet and alternative media censorship in communist countries like China, which has some of the most sophisticated internet-blocking technology in the world. But as the international stage is slow to catch up with governing activities taken on the Internet, the government-sponsored Internet blocking in China is imperfect, and people who know how to get around the system tend to be able to do it rather easily. It brings to light the questions not only of what people access on the Internet but where they access the Internet and which areas are easier for the government to control.

> *"Between March and September 2011, six Ethiopian journalists were arrested and charged with aiding terrorism."*

Restrictions on Media Undermine Democracy

Barbara Unmüßig

In the following viewpoint, Barbara Unmüßig discusses the unfortunate trend in which governments all over the world attempt to shut down actions taken by any and all civil society actors. In the last 25 years, governments in Africa, Asia, Latin America, and the Middle East have taken more and more drastic actions against civil rights protest, a crucial threat to the spread of democracy. And while the vilification of civil society is nothing new, people have been denied their fundamental rights of freedom of assembly, association, and speech to no or very little consequence. Unmüßig is president of the Heinrich Böll Foundation.

As you read, consider the following questions:

1. Why do autocratic countries strive to shut down any forms of public protest?
2. Why is freedom of the press crucial for democratic governments?
3. Why did the author's organization withdraw from Ethiopia?

A disconcerting trend has been perceptible for quite some time. Governments across all continents—irrespective of their political orientation—are taking drastic action against civil society actors: against non-governmental organizations, social and ecological activists, women's rights activists and human rights advocates. The space for actors who are critical of government policies, who call for democracy and human rights, who take an active stand against large-scale projects, and who protest against social injustice, land grabbing and environmental degradation is shrinking. These actors are increasingly the focus of state and private powers and the target of vilification campaigns, repression or criminalization. As a political foundation with its roots firmly planted in the civil societies of our partner countries, we have experienced first-hand how their space is being restricted (shrinking spaces) or how it is becoming virtually impossible for them to carry out their political activities (closing spaces). An independent and critical civil society is not just a thorn in the side of a multitude of governments in Africa, Asia, Latin America and the Middle East; these same governments are fighting civil society to an extent unheard of in the past 25 years.

Civil Society: No Thank You

Intimidating, vilifying or even banning civil society is nothing new. Many people have been denied the fundamental rights of freedom of assembly, association and speech that are entrenched in the Universal Declaration of Human Rights of 1948, and this denial continues even today. We have even seen setbacks for quite some time: the space granted civil society actors to carry out their activities is being massively restricted. This is not only true of authoritarian or semi-authoritarian regimes but also of democratic governments. Some of the advances made in democratization in Eastern Europe, Africa and Latin America in the aftermath of the Cold War are just taken back. The rights to participation and involvement are being taken away again. What is more, an increasing number of nations are jointly embarking on an outright "counter-offensive" against active citizenship.

Dozens of countries in Africa, Asia, Latin America, Eastern Europe and the Middle East have long since thwarted external democracy promotion—whether governmental or non-governmental. They do this with a veritable bundle of measures: comprising laws, bureaucratic and tax regulations and harassment, smear campaigns in the media, secret service methods and open repression. There appears to be an open season on the types of restriction that are permitted: activists are arrested, bank accounts frozen, threats made, licenses revoked, websites blocked, registrations coerced and offices closed.

From "Foreign Agents" and "Softer Aggression"

2006 saw the introduction of a new NGO law in Russia. In 2012 —Vladimir Putin had just returned to power in the Kremlin— every organization that "received money from abroad" and "was politically active" was obliged to register as a "foreign agent". Since virtually none of them complied with this obligation, the law was amended in 2014 to permit the state to register an organization in this list against its will. So those not labeling their materials as a "foreign agent", a term that most people in Russia associate with spies and enemies, can expect to be hit with a huge fine. Since 2015, it is also possible to declare foreign NGOs "undesirable". A total of twelve (largely US) organizations have been added to the "patriotic stop list" by the Federation Council, the upper house of Russia's Federal Assembly. The Council claimed that their activities showed signs of "mild aggression" against Russia. According to the Chairman of the Foreign Affairs Committee, Kosachov, these foundations are solely interested in priming people for mass street protests that they can activate "when they decided the time has come". The National Endowment for Democracy was the first NGO to be virtually expelled by the Attorney General in late July 2015.

China evidently also perceives the presence of foreign civil society organizations as a security risk: a fifth column threatening social stability and perhaps even the longevity of China's government. The second draft published at the beginning of May 2015 governing foreign NGOs stipulates that virtually every organization is required to register with the security authorities. They are said to be responsible for administrative tasks and control. Moreover, foreign organizations will require a domestic patron who is to be vested with responsibility for every activity undertaken by the international NGOs. All activities are expected to be forbidden that are of a "political and religious" nature, that "compromise internal security", or violate "concepts of social morality". The deliberately vaguely worded definitions and content leave plenty of space for arbitrary interpretation. If the law were to be passed as it stands now, Chinese organizations would no longer be allowed to receive money from foreign organizations, if their offices or their activities are not registered and approved.

Smaller nations have been equally swift in making it clear that they will not tolerate any "color revolutions": there will be "no rose, orange, or even banana revolution", the President of Belarus, Lukashenko, is quoted as saying in 2005, who is still in office today. Ethiopia's President Meles Zenawi also held a television address to announce that there will be no rose or green revolution in Ethiopia and proceeded to push through a law in 2009 prohibiting politically active NGOs from acquiring more than ten percent of their funding from abroad. The country's open political landscape has ceased to exist. All 547 members of parliament elected in 2015 belong to the ruling political party, the Ethiopian People's Revolutionary Democratic Front (EPRFD).

This bad practice is also catching on in Europe: since 2014, the government in Hungary has been taking action against organizations that receive financial support from "EEA and Norway Grants", a fund that opposes social and economic inequality in Eastern Europe and is primarily funded by Norway. In July 2014, Prime Minister Orbán warned against "political activists who are getting paid from abroad" and who are "advancing foreign interests in Hungary". Stigmatizing rhetoric is deployed with the specific aim of discrediting the work of NGOs critical of the government. In 2014, the governmental agency KEHI launched a criminal probe into NGOs that had either received financial aid from Norway or passed it on to Hungarian NGOs, including numerous reputable organizations such as the Ökotárs Foundation.

Where Does This Sense of Threat Emanate?

An increasing number of governments perceive NGOs as an extension of Western governments, as a danger for political, economic and social control over their own country. Katja Drinhausen and Günter Schucher from the German Institute for Global and Area Studies (GIGA) reason this shift with the foreign policy pursued by G.W. Bush, interventions in Afghanistan and Iraq (regime change), and the West's declarations of solidarity with the color revolutions in Georgia, Ukraine and Central Asia, as well as the revolutions in the Middle East from 2011 onwards.

Government resistance to external democracy promotion is, above all, justified in its eyes by the country's "sovereignty"—a key category in international law—that has attained a high emotional importance in many countries as a result of the decolonization struggles. Looked at from this perspective, democratization aid is viewed as an illicit intervention into the internal affairs of another state. The bugbear of the "color revolutions" plays a major role here—regime change in the early 2000s—that were named after symbolically related colors or fragrant plants.

Developments of this nature are very troublesome to us. Sounding out the political space for action in a difficult environment is just one of the core activities of a political foundation. The number of strategies available to international organizations here is few and far between given such an environment. Weighing these requires a sure instinct and responsible gauging as to whether the safety of the cooperation partners and staff is ensured. This sometimes means remaining in the country despite every form of resistance that is presented, "hibernating" there, and supporting and assisting civil society actors for as long as possible or until the space widens again. Being present in a country can signify that the room for discussion with partners can be held open, and sometimes prevents partners from having to end their activities immediately or being arrested, and that the existence of the organizations can be extended somewhat. Staying in a country can mean that organizations need to restrict themselves to certain topics and rescind political visibility.

Sometimes, however, it also entails having to draw consequences and withdrawing from a country if the space afforded to them is shrinking to zero. It is for this reason that we withdrew from Ethiopia towards the end of 2012. The freedom of press, opinion and association had become dramatically restricted there over the past few years. The passing of laws on the role and functions of NGOs in 2009 as well as the implementation regulations of autumn 2011 reached new heights in political control and restrictions on the freedom to act.

Ethiopia—Closing Spaces for Civil Society

Between March and September 2011, six Ethiopian journalists were arrested and charged with aiding terrorism; a further six journalists were tried in their absence. In December 2011, two Swedish journalists were sentenced to eleven years in prison, while two Ethiopian journalists were imprisoned to 14 years each in January 2012, and an exiled blogger was handed down a lifelong jail sentence. In June 2012, renowned journalist Eskinder Nega along with 23 other people were found guilty of terrorist acts and also given long or life sentences. Critical journalists have, for years, felt that they had been pressurized and that their safety had been compromised. A number of newspapers were discontinued (e.g. Addis Neger in 2009, Awramba Times in 2011), and many critical journalists have fled the country before they would have faced charges. Argaw Ashine, the Chairman of the Ethiopian Environment Journalist Association and a long-standing partner of the Heinrich Böll Foundation, left the country in 2011 after his name had been cited in a report from the US embassy in Ethiopia published by WikiLeaks.

A draft text submitted by the Ethiopian government in April 2012 ultimately confirmed that independent political work would not be possible even after the conclusion of a bilateral agreement and that the means left available to the Heinrich Böll Foundation would have been extremely limited. For example, the law prohibits any and every form of women's rights or human rights activity. Moreover, existing and potential partner organizations continue to be subjected to the regulations of the NGO law and therefore do not perform the core activities of the Foundation. Civil society is thus denied political role and consequently reduced to implementing the government's goals. The consequence of this is depolitization and self-censorship. The Foundation was unable to find any other partner organizations capable or willing to hold up to this development.

What's Next?

The fact that critical voices campaigning on behalf of human rights and rule of law as well as LGBTI rights and an economic policy geared towards social and ecological justice are a source of disapproval to those in power is nothing new. What is new, however, is the massive and shameless way in which they seek to counteract this—a development that will endure and may even worsen. Therefore, the massive restrictions placed on the space afforded civil societies must be put on the political agenda. Freedom of opinion, organization and association are the essence of any democracy. Their restriction poses a challenge to democratic governments and global cooperation. This issue must therefore become part of foreign and development policy as well as human rights discussions, be taken up by governments, and, globally, be integrated into inter-governmental discussions and negotiations.

> "It is a fundamental human right to use and access the Internet to … share ideas and solutions, and learn about the many diverse cultures in the world."

Human Rights Are at Stake on the Internet

Hamza Ben Mehrez

In the following viewpoint, Hamza Ben Mehrez addresses the roundtable discussions in Amman, Jordan, hosted by the Humanist Institute for Cooperation with Developing Countries (HIVOS). The community discussed human rights, access and infrastructure, and the promotion of policy practices in an event titled "Human Rights on the Internet, What's at Stake?" This event also discussed the challenges and issues regarding online rights and the changes that must be made to ensure free and open Internet access for all citizens living in developing countries. Ben Mehrez is an Internet policy analyst of HIVOS foundation on IGMENA, a program that brings together voices from the Arab region on Internet governance and policy.

As you read, consider the following questions:

1. What are the long-term consequences of governments attempting to restrict Internet access?
2. Why is it fundamentally important that all countries deploy a sustainable infrastructure for Internet access?
3. In countries like Jordan, the government controls which websites can be licensed. How does this negatively affect the rights of Jordanian citizens who attempt to utilize the Internet?

O n Wednesday, 29 June 2016, the Humanist Institute for Cooperation with Developing Countries (HIVOS) organized a roundtable discussion in Amman, Jordan. Thirty participants from the wider Internet Governance (IG) and IGMENA community attended a regional policy discussion with partners, staff, and participants to think together on issues related to IG, human rights, access and infrastructure, and the promotion of policy practices on the ground. The event was entitled "Human Rights on the Internet, What's at Stake?" The first session discussed Internet infrastructure, standards, and regulations and the second session discussed human rights, online freedoms, policies, and the challenges lying ahead.

Internet Governance, Infrastructure, and Access

The first workshop was moderated by Ms. Ahlam Abu-Jadallah, Head of the National Domain Names Section at the National Information Technology Center (NITC). Ms. Abu-Jadallah kicked off a discussion on the situation of Internet calls and applications such as VoIP and OTT in Jordan, specifically the attempts made by the local community to stop the Telecommunication Regulatory Commission's (TRC) intention to introduce taxation on the cost of Internet calls in Jordan. In the same vein, participants mentioned that there might be another reason behind this decision, which was originally made not only because of the financial loss suffered by the service providers (ISPs), but also as a new form of censorship imposed by the regulator on Internet usage, allegedly because of the surrounding political environment and high-level national security issues in the region.

Mr. Fahd Batayneh, Stakeholder Engagement Manager for the Middle East at ICANN, mentioned that there is an increase in Internet penetration and a rise in the adoption of smartphones, which has led to a decline in sending text messages and making voice calls, especially international voice calls. Participants in the roundtable discussion mentioned that there is a notable drop in international voice calls. According to the latest figures by the TRC, there are more than 6.3 million Internet users in Jordan and some 13 million active mobile subscriptions. Figures by the ICT Ministry indicate that smartphone penetration in Jordan exceeds 70 percent. The good news is that no charges will be imposed in Jordan on the use of Voice over Internet Protocol (VoIP) services such as Skype and Viber.

Mr. Walid Al Khatib, Ph.D., of Yarmouk University, added that according to estimates by experts in the field, there are more than 3 million WhatsApp users in Jordan. Experts have repeatedly stressed that it is difficult and unrealistic to impose fees on such services, as there are technological solutions to bypass any blockage and many alternatives to these apps online. He mentioned that several social media activists have been leading online campaigns to protest against any plans to impose fees on such apps, after reports said the Kingdom's telecom companies were considering the move. Other participants added that by the end of 2015, there were 13.7 million mobile subscriptions in the Kingdom, in addition to 7.9 million Internet users, according to the TRC. One of the recommendations was built around a strong VoIP business model that, in order to survive, should rely on marketing research and strong communication of new services based on market demand, great customer service, and impeccable technical support.

Mrs. Rana Hourani, a lawyer and data protection specialist, talked about the recent blocking of some Internet applications and services during a specific period, such as high school exams, and their impact on citizens and users in general. This policy has been followed in more than one country, such as Iraq and Algeria, in addition to Jordan, to get a safe exam environment free of different methods of cheating. She approached the issue from a legal perspective, by pointing out that the policy is not effective and will have negative consequences on the climate of online freedoms in the long term. She added that the victims of blocking for some services or publications or legally pursued do not conflict with the Penal Code and the law of cybercrime, which was recently passed in Jordan. This situation can create negative prospects for the future of online freedoms and human rights.

In the same context, Mr. Batayneh agreed that blocking these services during the exam period was not the most optimal solution and that those involved had to look into other methods to solve the whole problem of cheating on high school exams. Suggestions of going back to the grassroots of this whole "horror show" is a good starting point.

Ms. Asma Salem, Systems Engineer at the National Information Technology Center, mentioned that Internet access is the most important element to achieve a technological revolution in Jordan. However, positive developments are occurring for both Jordan's fixed and mobile broadband sectors in 2016. Jordan is trying to build and enhance Internet infrastructure and utilize services related to the Internet such as e-commerce, information connectivity, accessibility, etc. There is a fundamental need to deploy a sustainable infrastructure that supports the expansion of the Internet in all vital sectors. The current infrastructure must maintain its survival. In other words, it needs to expand, decentralize, and grow to cover poor rural areas. More importantly, it must emphasize security and the protection of end users' private information, particularly with new waves of technological development such as the Internet of things (IoT). There still some restrictions to access websites during working hours in governmental institutions, which are quite different when using the Internet at home or in public places for free.

Mr. Alaa Al Radi, an IPv6 certified trainer, talked about IPv6 by claiming that it is much better than IPv4, which begs the question of why adoption hasn't been more widespread. Mr. Al Radi mentioned that IPv4 addresses are a limited resource that is expected to be exhausted in the near future. IANA will exhaust this pool in less than a year, with the Regional Internet Registries (RIRs) allocating all their remaining blocks back in January 2012. IPv6 is the next generation IP protocol, which will solve the address exhaustion problem. The discussion was then extrapolated to Internet Service Providers (ISPs) in Jordan, which need to take steps to ensure service continuity and transparency to customers at all times during transition and coexistence of the two protocols.

Other participants mentioned that ISPs in Jordan have managed to continue to provide new IPv4 addresses by reallocating some of the addresses they had assigned in the past but perhaps had never passed on to customers. This buys them a little more time while they scramble to roll out and support IPv6 addresses. All ISPs are faced with providing a migration path from IPv4 to IPv6 for all of their customers and they are currently working to ensure that the impact on their customers will be minimal. The reality is that most ISPs are saying that their customers will not be impacted by IPv4 address depletion "in the near term," which makes it sound as if they might be affected somehow and in some way sooner or later.

Internet Governance and Human Rights Policies

The second workshop was moderated by Mr. Hamza Ben Mehrez, IGMENA Lead Policy Analyst. Mrs. Rima Moquattach, Ph.D. English and Comparative Literature at the University of Jordan, took the lead in the discussion by discussing the importance of end users' awareness and education on their rights and freedoms on the Internet. It should not be inconsistent with internationally recognized human rights standards.

In Jordan, websites are licensed, censored, or blocked. Mrs. Moquattach asked: What is the procedure for licensing? What are the criteria to get a license? Is it easy? Who is responsible for this? She stated that we need to educate students how to gain from the Internet knowledge and experiences. It is a fundamental human right to use and access the Internet to participate in chat rooms, share ideas and solutions, and learn about the many diverse cultures in the world. While the Internet does a lot for students, there are also benefits for parents, teachers, and policy makers.

Mr. Yousef Alsarairah, former Director of the Security Department at the NITC and PSD, added a perspective on cybercrime law and the criminalization of a variety of hacking and cyber-related crimes in Jordan. The law provides a legal base for dealing with a variety of credit card and electronic banking scams. As such, it provides the punishments to be imposed on anyone who illegally obtains information about credit cards or financial transactions without just cause, or uses the same to obtain a benefit for himself or another person. Moreover, the law provides that anyone who intentionally enters into a website or information system without the proper permits shall be punished by a fine and/ or imprisonment. The penalty is increased with regards to any entry made (whether legally or illegally) with the intent to copy, delete, or in any other way alter the website itself, or any data it contains; or if the entry was made with the intent to impersonate the website's owner.

Some participants expressed their concerns on the punitive aspect of the cybercrime law in Jordan, its relation to defamation of public figures, and the criminalization of hackers because they represent a threat to national security and the anti-terrorism law. But who set the legal boundaries, extra-legality, and applicability of legal sentences or conviction? Attendees also discussed some of the issues of defamation that have occurred recently that touched known public figures, as well the lack of clear interpretation of the law that defines prohibited and permitted free speech to express critical opinion toward decision-makers, despite the

Net Neutrality

History has proven that every time government takes a market segment away from the public, the product ultimately costs more, performs worse, is harder to get, and ends up profiting a select few well-connected cronies at taxpayer expense.

If the FCC takes control of our internet service, there is risk—perhaps likelihood—that competing ISPs will be pared down to a select few "winning" vendors. Is it any wonder that Comcast, owner of the blatantly pro-big government news channel MSNBC, and one of the largest contributors to the Obama campaign, is a full-throated supporter of the net neutrality bill?

In these kinds of quid pro quo arrangements, make no mistake: the deep-pockets federal government trades cash for control. And the cash is non-partisan. There's a net neutrality bill floating around Congress, and sponsors Fred Upton (R-MI) and Greg Walden (R-OR) received hefty contributions from telecom companies.

Chinese internet users know that their every keystroke is monitored by the government. They live behind a digital "Iron Curtain," justified by the need for a "healthy internet." According to Reporters Without Borders, web users and bloggers who stray from the party line are routinely arrested and imprisoned.

There is a price to pay for government-enforced fairness and safety. And there is no proposed government improvement to internet service that would not be accomplished faster and better by competition in the free market.

The internet may seem to be a ubiquitous benefit to us all, just there for the taking. Actually, each component of the internet originated and continues to operate in the free market as a competitive for-profit business opportunity.

Free market versus government bureaucracy and control? If we want the best internet service and access for all of us in the People's Republic of America, this is not even a fair fight.

"China Has Net Neutrality: Government Control of Internet Coming to America Too," by Tom Balek, Franklin Center for Government & Public Integrity, February 23, 2015.

presence of competent judges, law specialists, and policy experts in cybersecurity and cybercrime.

Mr. Huthaifa Bustanji, Judicial Assistant in the Judicial Inspection Department of the Ministry of Justice, mentioned that the domain name system (DNS) has been developed in the recent years, but there are many concerns, and the system still constitutes a big challenge to stakeholders and decision makers in Jordan. The Jordanian constitution introduces human rights and freedom of expression, and leaves the door open for legal interpretation for determining the nature of practicing these rights. In this regard, neither the Jordanian National Information Technology Center nor the Jordanian legal system have clarified human rights on the Internet. Therefore, new laws shall include the right of privacy, data protection, net neutrality, and the right of freedom of expression.

Mr. Abed M. Khatib, from AlNajeh (NGO), mentioned that Jordan has a highly critical Internet censorship environment, especially after the so-called "Arab Uprising." It came as a need to clamp down on young activists' opinions and to avoid any kind of speeches that criticize the government or promote radical thoughts. Meanwhile, the government must identify and understand the difference between "hate speech" and "freedom of expression" in order to guarantee more freedom on the Internet without any governmental control. For example, the most known aspect of the Press and Publications Law is the requirement for Jordanian news websites to obtain a government license, or else face blocking by Internet Service Providers as a first step before legal procedures are taken to shut down the website's operations. But this is only part of a bigger and more complex picture. According to the Press and Publications Law, the Director of the Jordanian Media Commission has the personal authority to decide which websites in Jordan qualify as news websites. Mr. Khatib stated that a certain "legal vagueness" is used to interpret what website is legitimate or illegitimate to operate when it comes to the internal or external affairs of the Kingdom.

Mr. Khatib believes that the Internet is a wide space where everyone has the right to post, share, and deal with content whatever the content is. The main challenge is to convince stakeholders, such as the ISPs and governments, that universal access should be allowed and limitations must not be applied. As an example, if you are connected to a Jordanian university's Wi-Fi and searched for a term such as "sex genotype," your access to this information will be denied because of the term "sex" in your search. The government, private sector, and education facilities share this limitation on Internet access, which is related to rights disclosure. And not only does the law require news websites to have a full-time Editor-In-Chief who has been a member of the Jordan Press Association for at least four years, but membership in the association is not guaranteed, and a large number of professional journalists in Jordan do not meet the membership requirements.

Mr. Batayneh stated that he believes a user can define his/her own levels of privacy. He brought up the example of posting on social media and the concept of sharing without consent from the original poster of a picture or content. Who is to be blamed here when privacy is infringed? He also brought up the notion of "posting diplomatically," where bloggers who want to post content criticizing someone or something can stay away from "pointing fingers directly" and phrasing things in a diplomatic manner. This can keep many away from any possible trouble. Finally, he spoke about surveillance and privacy. He did mention that while privacy is important, can lack surveillance keep us safe from the likes of ISIL and all the conspiracies happening around us? Do we want to live safely, or do we want to live freely?

Mr. Hamza Salem, Computer Engineer, Developer, and Audio blogger, talked about how free speech became a serious issue when the concept shifted to the Internet. "Everything is documented, collected, stored, and sold." This is the most complex thing in the relationship between free speech and documented speech on the Internet. There is a gap between the technology and the law because policies and laws related to broadcasting (websites, radio, etc.) are vaguely and ambiguously defined, maybe intentionally by the lawyers and jurists who work in this field.

Terms and conditions are too complex and push the end users to ignore reading and understanding complex technical and legal clauses. Moreover, the terms and conditions of the Internet governance of big companies (like Google) are not well defined. There is a corporate responsibility, government responsibility, end user responsibility to talk about complex topics (deep web, ethical algorithms) to make new flexible rules, create easy-to-understand terms of service to avoid government censorship, metadata collection, and corporate censorship that transcends national laws.

Finally, participants discussed tools used to bypass blocked sites as well as circumvention methods such as VPNs and ToR. One for the fundamental recommendations of the meeting was that technology users need to be aware that not everyone has the same opportunities when it comes to technology and the understanding of the need for online security. Working toward equal digital rights and supporting electronic access is the starting point of "digital citizenship" in Jordan.Digital exclusion makes it difficult to grow as a society when some people are increasingly using these tools. Helping to provide and expand access to technology, not only in Jordan but in the MENA region as a whole, should be a goal of all digital citizens. End users in Jordan need to keep in mind that there are some that may have limited access, so other resources may need to be provided. To become productive citizens, we need to be committed to making sure that no one is denied human rights on the Internet; this is what is at stake.

> *"The September 11 attacks illustrated that terrorism crosses national and ethnic boundaries and changed the prevailing attitudes to terrorism."*

Cyber Terrorism Is on the Rise

Fawzia Cassim

In the following excerpted viewpoint, Fawzia Cassim discusses the growth of cyber terrorism and concludes that it will continue to be a threat into the future. Since this is a global issue, it must take a global response to curb it. Terrorism is no longer solely the drastic actions like those taken on 9/11. Cyber terrorism is a recognized cyber crime, but there is very little legal framework available on either a national or international level to combat it. Due to the Internet's rapid growth, acts to safeguard it are lacking and will continue to be exploited by terrorists until it can be remedied at an international level. Cassim is associate professor, Department of Criminal and Procedural Law, University of South Africa.

As you read, consider the following questions:

1. Why is the cyber world conducive for terrorist activity?
2. What is the difference between "hacktivism" and "cyber terrorism"?
3. What are the similarities and differences in actions taken by the US, UK, and India to address cyber terrorism?

Cyber space is regarded as the meeting place for criminal groups.[1] Cyber space has recently emerged as the latest battleground in this digital age.[2] The convergence of the physical and virtual worlds has resulted in the creation of a "new threat" called cyber terrorism.[3] Before 9/11, much apprehension arose about the threat of cyber terrorism including fears about a "digital Pearl Harbour".[4] The millennium bug further enhanced this fear. [5] In the context of post 9/11, the threat of cyber terrorism is often linked to Al- Qaeda and other terrorist organisations.[6] Cyber terrorists are regarded as computer savvy individuals who look for vulnerabilities that can be easily exploited.[7] Cyber terrorism is one of the recognised cyber crimes.[8] It has been defined as the "premeditated use of disruptive activities, or the threat thereof, in cyber space, with the intention to further social, ideological, religious, political or similar objectives, or to intimidate any person in the furtherance of such objectives.[9] Usually such attacks can take different forms: a terrorist could break into a company's computer network causing havoc, sabotage a country's gas lines or wreak havoc on the international finance system.[10] These terrorist attacks against information infrastructures, computer systems, computer programmes and data may cause injury, loss of life and destruction of property. The aim of such unlawful attacks is to intimidate or persuade a government or its people to further a political or social objective.[11] Cyber attack methods are also said to possess many advantages over conventional methods of terrorism.[12] However, distinctions should be drawn between hacktivism and cyber terrorism, and the use of digital means for organisational purposes and the use of digital communications to actually commit acts of terror.[13]

The horrific events of 9/11 provided the impetus for many countries to introduce anti-terrorist legislation. Such anti- terrorist legislation not only focuses on legislation to criminalise cyber terrorist activity and impose penalties proportional to the act but also to prevent cyber terrorist activity or mitigate its impact by denying cyber terrorists materials, finance, support and equipment. The September 11 attacks illustrated that terrorism crosses national and ethnic boundaries and changed the prevailing attitudes to terrorism.[14] Indeed, after 9/11, the discussion about cyber security and cyber terrorism took centre stage.[15] The United States of America introduced the Patriot Act of 2001 in response to the 9/11 attacks on its soil. The United Kingdom has introduced a number of anti-terrorist legislation, namely, the Terrorism Act of 2000, the Anti-Terrorism, Crime and Security Act 2001 and the Terrorism Act of 2006. The Information Technology Amendment Act of 2008 in India contains a provision on cyber terrorism. South Africa has introduced a number of legislative measures to address the growing threat of cyber terrorism and terrorist financing such as the Prevention of Organised Crime Act 38 of 1999 ("POCA"), the Financial Intelligence Centre Act 38 of 2001 ("FICA"), the Electronic Communications and Transactions Act 25 of 2002 ("ECT), the Regulation of Interception of Communications and Provision of Communications-Related Information Act 70 of 2002 ("RICA") and the Protection of Constitutional Democracy against Terrorism and Related Activities Act 33 of 2004 ("PCDTRA").[16]

The article examines the definition of cyber terrorism and different uses of the Internet by terrorist groups. The article also looks at measures introduced in the United States of America, United Kingdom and India to address the threat posed by cyber terrorism. The South African position is also examined. The study reveals that some confusion exists between the terms "hacktivism" and "cyber terrorism". This confusion together with media-induced fears about imminent threats about cyber terrorism has exaggerated the threat of cyber terrorism. Nevertheless, the study also demonstrates that while cyber terrorism does not pose an imminent threat, this could change in the near future. Therefore, the threat posed by cyber terrorism should not be taken lightly. To this end, proper and effective measures should be put in place to counteract such threats in the future. The article also contends that while the global fight against cyber terrorism is necessary, measures addressing cyber terrorism should not jeopardise basic human rights and fundamental freedoms. Therefore, countries need to ensure that a balance is maintained between the protection of human rights and the need for effective prosecution when enacting cyber terrorist legislation.

Definition of Cyber Terrorism

Terrorists are said to use the Internet to spread propaganda and conduct internal communications. However, threats resulting from terrorist use of the Internet have been strongly debated. According to Phillip Brunst, the difference in opinion is due to a lack of exact terminology about the term "cyber terrorism".[17] Maura Conway defines cyber terrorism as "acts of terrorism carried out using the Internet and /or against Internet infrastructures".[18] Dorothy Denning defines cyber terrorism as "the convergence of terrorism and cyberspace. It is understood to mean unlawful attacks and threats of attack against computers, networks and the information stored therein when done to intimidate or coerce a government or its people in the furtherance of political or social objectives".[19] Mark Pollit defines cyber terrorism as a "premeditated, politically motivated attack against information, computer systems, computer programmes, and data which result in violence against noncombatant targets by sub national groups or clandestine agents".[20] Such attacks may lead to death or bodily injury, or cause explosions, plane crashes, water contamination, severe economic loss or serious attacks against critical infrastructure.[21] Cyber terrorism encompasses attacks against life and electronic infrastructure which are directed against national security establishments and critical infrastructure.[22] The aim of the attacks is to cause a state of terror and panic in the general public. Terrorists may also use information technology to perpetrate new offences or exploit cyberspace to commit more traditional activities such as planning, intelligence, logistical capabilities and finance.[23] Thus, terrorists may use computer technology to secure many of their organisational goals. However, attacks that disrupt nonessential services or present a costly nuisance do not amount to cyber terrorism.[24] Denning also maintains that while terrorists may use cyberspace to facilitate traditional forms of terrorism such as bombings, or use the Internet to spread their messages and recruit supporters, there are few indications that they are actually pursuing cyber terrorism.[25] However, this could change in the future.

The blurring of the distinction between hacktivism and cyber terrorism has also fuelled the debate on cyber terrorism. The term "hacking" refers to the use of special software and techniques of a disruptive nature ('hacking tools') to exploit computers.[26] However, Peter Krapp maintains that hacktivists should not be regarded as secret agents, soldiers, terrorists or net warriors but rather as individuals or groups who strive to capture attention and achieve maximum media effect in their quest to raise the awareness of citizens regarding certain rights and liberties.[27] It is debatable whether hacktivists will succeed in changing government policy.[28] Nevertheless, hacktivism should be distinguished from cyber terrorism.

Different Uses of the Internet by Terrorist Groups

Organised crime and terrorist groups are using sophisticated computer technology to bypass government detection and carry out destructive acts of violence. The actions of Rami Yousef who orchestrated the 1993 World Trade Center bombing by using encryption to store details of his scheme on his laptop computer, is a case in point.[29] It has also been reported that the first known attack by terrorists against a country's computer system took place in Sri Lanka in 1998, when the ethnic Tamil Tigers guerrillas overwhelmed Sri Lankan embassies with 800 e-mails a day over a two-week period.[30] These messages threatened massive disruption of communications, and caused fear and panic among ordinary Sri

Lankans as the rebel group was notorious for killing people. During the war in Kosovo in 1999, Serb sympathisers tried to target the NATO website with viruses.[31] In another incident, cyber attacks were launched against the Estonian state during April 2007. The targets were the Estonian Parliament, banks, media houses and government departments. These attacks affected critical services.[32] The events in Estonia illustrated how countries can be put at risk by attacks via the Internet.[33] Thus computers have been used as tools by terrorists to execute terror attacks and advance their particular agendas.[34] However, there is "little concrete evidence" to demonstrate that cyber terrorism has resulted in a catastrophic loss of life or physical destruction often associated with conventional terrorism.[35]

On the other hand, terrorists can also use the Internet for organisational purposes rather than to commit acts of terror. Terrorists can use the computer to commit various crimes such as identity theft, computer viruses, hacking, malware, destruction or manipulation of data.[36] Terrorists can use information communication technologies (ICTs) and the Internet for different purposes: propaganda, information gathering, preparation of real-world attacks, publication of training material, communication, terrorist financing and attacks against critical infrastructures.[37] This means that organisations or governments which depend on the operation of computers and computer networks can be easily attacked. The Internet has the advantage of being "a more immediate, individual, dynamic, in-depth, interactive, anonymous, unedited, cheaper and far-reaching process than conventional media".[38] These factors facilitate the task of terrorists to execute their plans unhindered.[39] Information on how to make bombs is also freely available on the Internet.[40] However, it should be borne in mind that "terrorist use of computers as a facilitator of their activities, whether for propaganda, recruitment, communication or other purposes is simply not cyber terrorism".[41] Similarly, protest action by way of" virtual sit-ins" on web sites (called electronic civil disobedience) does not amount to cyber terrorism.[42]

Cyber Terrorism: Myth or Reality?

Although cyber terrorism has become a more dominant force in the global battle between information and network warfare, much misconception still exists over what cyber terrorism entails. As stated earlier, it is important to recognise that all "cyberspace-based threats" are not necessarily terrorism.[43] According to Stohl, the concern with the threat of cyber terrorism stems from a combination of fear and ignorance.[44] Stohl maintains that the discussion about cyber security also involves some misinformation and the exploitation of fears of the general public.[45] The failure to distinguish between hacktivism and cyber terrorism has also contributed to the fear and hype about the threat of cyber terrorism.[46] Some writers believe that the media has also exaggerated the possibility of cyber terrorist attacks causing much concern and panic in the public domain.[47] However, the number of potential targets and the lack of proper and adequate safeguards have also made addressing the threat a daunting task. One should also not underestimate the risk and potential of future threats.[48] Thus, a need arises for the re-examination of commonly held beliefs about the nature of computer systems and cyber terrorism.[49] To this end, measures to address cyber security, to introduce adequate cyber terrorist legislation and to make software safe and effective should be introduced. One should also bear in mind that the removal of technical information from the Internet (such as information on how to execute terror attacks), does not provide an adequate guarantee to safeguard the Internet as such material can be easily loaded onto offshore or other international severs.[50] Gordon and Ford maintain that an urgent need arises for the development of minimum standards of security for computer networks.[51] They also endorse the idea of negotiations to resolve long-standing disputes with terrorist groups, the careful use of surveillance techniques to gather information on terrorist communications and the sharing of information across various public and private sectors to combat terrorism.[52]

Concerns in the United States of America

Since September 11, concerns about cyber terrorism in the United States have multiplied.[53] The USA Patriot Act of 2001 was enacted by President George Bush in response to the 9/11 attacks on the World Trade Centre and Pentagon.[54] Although the USA Patriot Act addresses several issues, certain key provisions relate to cyber security and other computer concerns. To this end, the Act has eased restrictions on electronic surveillance to facilitate the capture of terrorists.[55] The Act also contains anti-money laundering provisions in order to prevent terrorists from achieving any financial gain from their actions.[56] The Patriot Act also includes terrorism and computer crimes on its list of offences.[57] However, the Act has been criticised for violating the civil rights of ordinary American citizens.[58]

Cyber terrorists are said to have the ability to cripple critical infrastructure such as communication, energy and government operations. Cell phones have also been used to track terrorists and to provide evidence against them.[59] Terrorist websites are also under increased surveillance since 9/11 to strengthen the fight against terrorism.[60] A call has also been made for the development of cyber intelligence as a better co-ordinated government discipline to predict computer-related threats and deter them.[61] A bill on cyber security is currently being debated by the US Senate.[62] The bill is aimed at the protection of critical infrastructure such as power and phone companies, water and treatment plants and wireless providers. The enactment of the USA Patriot Act and other measures taken by the American government demonstrates the government's commitment to combat international terrorism including cyber terrorism.

Recommendations and Conclusions

The debate about the threat that cyber terrorism poses will continue into the future. Cyber terrorism is a global menace which requires a united, global response. One should not underestimate the risks and potential of future threats. Countries must work together to introduce a set of core consensus crimes that can be enforceable against cyber criminals in any jurisdiction.[63] The events in Estonia during 2007 demonstrated that governments are vulnerable to attacks by digital means. Every state should enact legislation denying cyber terrorists 'safe havens' and safe places of operation. However, "law alone is insufficient; it must be buttressed with faithful enforcement and effective prevention strategies".[64] Therefore, it is also important to build defences against cyber criminals and cyber terrorists. The convergence of terrorism and the cyber world has created a new threat that has to be taken seriously.[65]

South Africa can learn from the approaches followed in other countries. We can take note of the United States initiative to develop and enhance cyber intelligence and cyber security measures in order to better predict computer-related threats and deter them and we can investigate the possibility of introducing a similar model to the National Technical Assistance Centre in the United Kingdom to counteract and avert potential cyber terrorist threats. It is noteworthy that South Africa has introduced RICA which can be used to track down cyber terrorists using cell phones to plan their illegal activities or agendas. However, South Africa should also follow the United States and the United Kingdom and ratify the ECCC as the treaty offers a global approach to the global problem of cyber terrorism.

Although attempts by countries such as the United States, United Kingdom, India and South Africa to address cyber terrorism are laudable, there is room for improvement. It is submitted that this problem can be addressed not only though enacting stringent legislation and enhancing cyber security measures but also through international cooperation. Although the global fight against cyber terrorism is necessary, combating cyber terrorism should not jeopardise basic human rights and fundamental freedoms. To this end, "the urge to restrict, prohibit and to curtail must be resisted".[66] Therefore, countries need to ensure that a balance is maintained between the protection of human rights and the need for effective prosecution. The following steps should be taken by countries to combat the spectre of cyber terrorism globally:

- Countries should ensure that its cyber terrorism legislation is compatible with international -human rights instruments. It appears that adequate legislation has been introduced by the South African government, the United States, the United Kingdom and India. While the protection of cyber systems is a major concern, this security should not prejudice the fundamental rights and freedoms enshrined in our Constitutions and human rights instruments.
- Countries should educate the public about the threat of cyber terrorism as vigilance is a key factor in addressing the potential threat of cyber terrorism. Users of the Internet should also be encouraged to adopt stronger security measures.
- The role of the media is critical in the fight against cyber terrorism. The media should follow a concise and sensible approach rather than exploit the fears of the ordinary public.
- Countries should regulate cyber cafés as these cafés are popular internet access points.
- Countries should explore the feasibility of introducing internet filtering measures to control access to websites that pose serious threats to their national security.
- Countries should introduce specialised law enforcement and training skills, and improve computer forensic capabilities. The respective governments must also initiate support and training within government, with the help of the private sector and international enterprises. Crime and corruption at various government departments should also be rooted out.
- Countries should develop cyber intelligence as a new and better co-ordinated government discipline to predict computer-related threats and deter them.
- Countries should enter into partnerships with other countries to provide technical and material support and increase cooperation among the intelligence agencies of different countries to facilitate exchange of sensitive information to

counter cyber terrorist threats. International cooperation is important to ensure the integrity of the Internet. There should also be cooperation to secure networks.

- Countries should encourage reconciliation and respect for diversity, and bridge gulfs between different countries in the broader international community to counteract terrorist threats. To this end, negotiations should be explored as a way to resolve long-standing disputes. A country should also engage all its citizens in its counter terrorist strategies.

- Countries should keep pace with evolving technology to counteract potential cyber terrorist threats. New technologies need to be developed and enhanced in the global fight against terrorism.

- Countries such as South Africa should follow the United States and the United Kingdom and ratify and accede to the ECCC to avoid becoming vulnerable to cyber terrorism. The Convention is also open to accession by non-member states.

Notes

1 Tushabe and Baryamureeba 2005 *World Academy of Science, Engineering and Technology* 66.

2 Veerasamy 2009 *4th International Conference on Information Warfare and Security* 26-27 March.

3 It should be noted that the physical world refers to the place where we live and function, whilst the virtual world refers to the place in which computer programmes function.

4 The term "electronic or digital Pearl Harbour" was first coined by a tech writer one Winn Schwartau in 1991. See further, Stohl 2006 *Crime Law and Social Change* http://ceps.anu.edu.au/publications /pdfs/stohl.

5 The millenium bug which is also referred to as the Y2K problem, was the result of an outdated programming system which had not accounted for the transition from 1999 to 2000. Of course, this problem soon came to pass without any major catastrophe. *Ibid.*

6 *Ibid.*

7 Raghavan 2003 *Journal of Law, Technology and Policy* 297.

8 It is important to distinguish between cyber crime and cyber terrorism. Cyber terrorism is usually restricted to activities which have a cyber component and the common components of terrorism. Therefore, it is submitted that a discussion of cyber terrorism cannot be divorced from a discussion of terrorism as the two concepts are linked together. This article will focus on cyber terrorism. However, it will also touch on terrorism where relevant.

9 Tushabe & Baryamureeba (n 1) 66-67. Also see Denning 2002 http://www/iwar.org.uk/cyberterror/resources/denning.htm.

10 Guru & Mahishwar "Terror networking" 71.

11 *Ibid.*

12 Terrorists find cyber attack methods to be cheaper than traditional methods; the actions can be difficult to track or trace; the actions can be done remotely anywhere in the world; a number of targets can be attacked effortlessly and it can affect a large number of people. See Garg "Cyber terrorism" 121. Also see Brunst 2010 "Terrorism and the Internet" 53-56.

13 See Stohl 2006 (n 4) 1. Also see Krapp 2005 *Grey Room Inc and Massachusetts Institute of Technology* 70-93.

14 Young 2006 *Boston College International and Comparative Law Review* 23-103 29.

15 Frauenheim 2002 http://news.cnet.com/2100-1001-977780.html?tag=fd_top.

16 It should be emphasised that these legislative measures do not refer to cyber terrorism specifically. However, they also contain measures or provisions to address terrorist financing and the protection of computer systems. The discussion on South Africa in section 6 will elaborate further.

17 Brunst also maintains that the use of additional terminology such as "digital Pearl Harbour", "electronic Waterloo" and "electronic Chernobyl" which focus on possible future attacks by terrorists, has further complicated matters. See Brunst (n 12) 51.

18 Conway 2007 "Terrorism and the New Media" 1.

19 Denning (n 9) 2. Stohl sees no reason to reject Denning's definition. See Stohl (n 4) 8. Also see Gordon & Ford 2002 http://www.symantec.com/avcenter/reference/cyberterrorism.

20 Pollit 1998 http://www.scribd.com/doc/ ; Also see Goodman & Brenner 2002 *International Journal of Law and Information Technology* 150. However, Phillip Brunst regards Pollit's definition as being a narrow definition of cyber terrorism. He maintains that a broad definition of cyber terrorism might include other forms of terrorist use of the Internet. See Brunst (n 12) 51.

21 Gordon & Ford (n 19) 4; Goodman & Brenner (n 20) 145; Denning (n 9) 2. Also see Brunst (n 12) 66.

22 Goodman & Brenner (n 20). Weimann maintains that cyber terrorism involves the use of computer networks tools to harm or shut down critical national infrastructures such as energy, transportation and government operations. Weimann 2005 *Studies in Conflict and Terrorism* 130.

23 *Ibid.*

24 Denning (n 9) 2.

25 Conventional terrorism is said to have a "greater dramatic effect" than cyber terrorism. Denning (n 9) 19-20; 22. Also see Stohl (n 4) 8; 11-13. However, Brunst reports that although many attacks have taken place, they have been kept confidential to avoid security lapses or breaches if such details were published. See Brunst (n 12) 53.

26 Hacktivism includes electronic civil disobedience. For more information, see Denning (n 9)12.

27 Krapp (n 13) 86-88. Also see Brunst (n 12) 56-57, regarding the blurring of the distinction between the terms "hacktivism" and "cyber terrorism."

28 Denning (n 9) 22.

29 Bazelon *et al* 2006 *The American Criminal Law Review* 306.

30 See Tushabe & Baryamureeba (n 1) 67; Also see Denning (n 9) 7. Also see Walker 2006 "Cyber - Terrorism: United Kingdom" 635.

31 Walker (n 30) 635. Chinese computer hackers also launched attacks on US web sites to protest against NATO's bombing of a Chinese embassy in Kosovo. See Krapp (n 13) 72.

32 See Veerasamy "Conceptual Framework" 4. Also see Brunst (n 12) 62.

33 Brunst (n 12) 52.

34 It has also been reported that computers and the Internet played a key role in the execution of the September 11 attacks in that computers were used to make travel plans and purchase air tickets. However, it is submitted that these acts can be distinguished from cyber terrorism in that computers are used here to plan acts of terror rather than to commit acts of terror. See Gordon & Ford (n 19) 4; also see Gerke 2009 "Understanding Cybercrime" http://www.itu.int/ITU-D/cyb/ cybersecurity/legislation/html.

35 Stohl (n 4) 2. Computers are said to be the means to achieve terrorist purposes rather than the objects of attack. See Walker (n 30) 636.

36 "Malware" is the distribution of malicious codes to disrupt computer networks. See Raghavan (n 7) 299-300 regarding the different types of attacks that can be brought against computer networks. Also see Gordon and Ford (n 19) 7.

37 Gerke (n 34) 52-57. Also see Brunst (n 12) 70-73; 74-75; Walker (n 30) 635-642 and Conway (n 18) 4-10.

38 Conway (n 18) 3-4.

39 Raghavan (n 7) 297. It should be stated that the general motivations to commit crimes via the Internet are: the lack of a definite physical location, the use of bandwidth and speed of third parties to perpetrate cyber crimes, the anonymity of cyberspace, the lack of physical borders or boundaries and the cost- benefit ratio. For detailed discussion about these issues, see Brunst (n 12) 53-56.

40 This includes material such as *The Terrorist's Handbook*, *How to Make Bomb: Book Two* and *The Anarchist's Cookbook*. See Walker (n 30) 645. The Internet also contains detailed instructions on how to establish underground organisations and execute terror attacks. See Conway (n 18) 17.

41 Weimann (n 22) 133. Attacks on critical infrastructure are said to fall under the domain of cyber terrorism. Also see Walker (n 30) 634.

42 For more information on electronic civil disobedience, see Dominguez 2008 *Third Text* 661-670.

43 For example, attacks on data contained within systems and programmes do not translate to "terrorist" acts. However, in some instances, the distinction between cyber crime (such as hacking) and cyber terrorism has also become blurred. See Brunst (n 12) 56-57.

44 This translates to a fear of technology and the fear of terrorism (both unknown factors). This results in the nature of cyber terrorism being misunderstood. Also see Embar-Seddon 2002 *American Behavioural Scientist* 1033-1043.

45 Stohl (n 4) 5. Also see Conway (n 18) 29.

46 Hacking refers to activities conducted online that aim to reveal, manipulate and exploit vunerabilities in computer operating systems and software. Also see Denning (n 9) 12.

47 Veerasamy (n 2) 1. Also see Green 2002 *Washington Monthly* http://www. washingtonmonthly.com/features/2001/0211.green.html 1-8. Also see Frauenheim (n 15) 2.

48 The lack of a large cyber attack by terrorists should not make one complacent. See Brunst (n 12) 75.

49 Gordon and Ford (n 19) 14.

50 Conway (n 18) 19.

51 Gordon and Ford (n 19) 12.

52 *Ibid.*

53 The September 11 hijackings led to an outcry that airliners are susceptible to cyber terrorism. See Green (n 47) 4.

54 The USA Patriot Act stands for: Uniting and Strengthening America by Providing Appropriate Tools Required to Intercept and Obstruct Terrorism. See Young (n 14) 75-76. Also Raghavan (n 7) 298; 304. The law protects the national infrastructure by easing the restrictions placed on electronic surveillance by amending provisions of the Computer Fraud and Abuse Act 1986 to increase penalties for cybercrimes.

55 The Act has expanded the powers of the federal government to combat terrorism in the area of surveillance and interception of communications; it provides for closer policing of financial transactions; it strengthens the anti-money laundering regulations to disrupt terrorist funding opportunities and it authorizes administrative detentions. See Young (n 14) 76. Alse see Raghavan (n 7) 305.

56 See ss 301-77. Raghavan (n 7) 305.

57 See s 814. The increase in vigilance against the threat of cyber terrorism has resulted in increased penalties for all forms of computer hacking including hacktivist activity. See Dominguez (n 42) 664.

58 To illustrate this, the expanded surveillance measure in the Act has been criticised because of its lack of adequate checks and balances. The government's ability to spy on suspected computer trespassers without a court order has also been criticised as it infringes on the civil liberties of suspected trespassers. Raghavan (n 7) 310.

59 Walker (n 30) 664. It is noteworthy that South Africa has introduced the Regulation of Interception of Communication Act 2002 (RICA) for this purpose. 60 Conway (n 18) 22-23; 28.

61 Anonymous 2011 http://www.eLaw@legalbrief.co.za.

62 See Anonymous 2012 http://www.csoonline.com/article/700397/liberman-cybersecurity-act-of-2012.

63 The new law requires all UK Internet companies to install hardware which will enable the Government Communication Headquarters to intercept any phone call or text message. See Jalalzai 2012 *The Daily Outlook*http://outlookafghanistan.net/topics. php?post_id=3833. Also see Anonymous 2012 http://www.elaw@legalbrief.co.za . 64 See Goodman & Brenner (n 20) 223.

65 See Young (n 14) 28.

66 See Brunst (n 12) 76.

> *"Digital technology allows satellites to transmit scores of channels where previously they could transmit only a few."*

Satellite Broadcasts Can Circumvent National Controls Around the World

Naomi Sakr

In the following viewpoint, Naomi Sakr discusses the development of satellite broadcasting companies that cater directly to those living in the Middle East. Because these companies are not located within the countries they service, they are able to circumvent much of the state-sponsored censorship and bring a wider worldview to those in non-democratic countries. Conversely, many of these satellite broadcasting companies are still owned by people or peoples who have a certain agenda that they want relayed to the consumers in these countries, therefore still leading to issues of state-sponsored propaganda and limited access depending on costs. Sakr worked as a Middle East specialist for the Economist *and currently is professor of Media Policy at University of Westminster in London.*

"Satellite Television and Development in the Middle East," by Naomi Sakr, Middle East Research and Information Project. Reprinted by permission. This article first appeared in *Middle East Report*, published by the Middle East Research & Information Project.

As you read, consider the following questions:

1. Of the satellite broadcasting companies listed in this viewpoint, why is Al Jazeera different from the others?
2. Why is it crucial for Middle East satellite broadcast companies to be developed within Middle Eastern countries, even though many of these satellite broadcast companies are located in Europe?
3. What are some of the current issues with access to satellite broadcast channels in the Middle East, and how can they be remedied?

Upon hearing a Dutch diplomat recite a dismal litany of statistics indicating the current social and economic plight of most Middle Eastern states, a Jordanian academic heaved a sigh. "This is a triple tragedy," she said. "Not only are the figures bad, but they have to be collated by foreign agencies while governments in the region keep people in the dark."

For human rights campaigners, the three tragedies are interlinked. Ideally, freedom of information should be a catalyst for all aspects of development by creating public awareness and encouraging transparent decision-making. Conversely, development should promote freedom of information by increasing the channels through which information flows. If this is the case, what are the implications of satellite television broadcasting for development in the Middle East? Although several Arab satellite broadcasters have been operating since the early 1990s, a sudden proliferation of new ventures since 1996 has inspired hope that the vicious circle of censorship and stagnation in the region might soon be broken.

By transcending borders, satellite broadcasts are technically capable of circumventing national controls. Several channels serving Middle Eastern audiences are based outside the region. [1] A quick glance at the six leading free-to-air Arabic-language operators, however, reveals that, where free speech is concerned, ownership matters more than location. The London-based Middle East Broadcasting Centre (MBC) belongs to Sheikh Walid bin Ibrahim al-Ibrahim, a brother-in-law of Saudi Arabia's King Fahd. The latter is widely believed to have underwritten a large part of MBC's costs.

The Egyptian Space Channel is part of an enormous state-run monopoly, the Egyptian Radio and Television Union, while Emirates Dubai Television is state-owned. Of the two private Lebanese channels that expanded into satellite television at the end of 1996, one—Future TV—is part-owned by Lebanon's former prime minister, Rafiq al-Hariri. The second, the Lebanese Broadcasting Corporation, is controlled by a board dominated by ministers and officials close to the Syrian government. Syrian military intelligence activities in Lebanon, in addition to the large number of Syrians currently watching Future TV and LBC, make trouble-free relations with Damascus a prerequisite for Lebanese media entrepreneurs.

If there is one exception to the rule of ownership by government or government proxy, the only candidate out of the six leading satellite broadcast channels is Al Jazeera, based in Qatar. Officially, this is an independent station, whose "only" connection to government is that it was promised five years' worth of government loans. Unofficially, Al Jazeera's output indicates that it has been given considerable scope. Its staff prioritize stories according to their newsworthiness, not their acceptability to local regimes, [2] and much of Al Jazeera's material is broadcast live. Newsworthiness criteria, however, are subjective, and Al Jazeera's criteria may well reflect the Qatari leadership's agenda for now. The paradox of Al Jazeera's situation is that if it were wholly in the private sector its relatively independent approach might be curtailed.

Al Jazeera's reputation for controversy while operating out of Doha rather than a European capital represents a breakthrough in media-related development in the Middle East. Along with LBC and the pay-TV provider, Orbit, Al-Jazeera has accelerated a trend towards live and compelling talk show programming that has obliged the older channels to keep up with the competition. Social development of this sort does not stem from purely political decisions, however. The economics and technology of satellite television play a more decisive role.

A Pan-Arab Market

As the number of channels has increased, so has demand for programs. As a rule of thumb, every channel requires approximately 7,000 hours of programming per year. In the case of digital operators such as Orbit or the other Saudi-backed pay-TV company, Arab Radio and Television, 7,000 hours of programs are needed for every channel in their digital "bouquet." Saudi Arabia's wireless cable system will eventually offer scores of channels; five of them were launched from scratch by MBC.

On one hand, demand on this scale has stimulated the growth of production centers in those cities where technical expertise is concentrated, notably Cairo, Beirut, Damascus and Amman. Although based in Europe, Orbit and MBC rely increasingly on studios in the Middle East, which offer cost savings. This trend encourages the independent sector and means that, with broadcasters seeking producers rather than the other way around, producers can afford to be bolder in dictating their terms.

On the other hand, the shift to indigenous program production is relatively recent, and it will take time for proper facilities to develop and expand. In the meantime, those with cash to spend on new studios are more likely to be members of the ruling establishments. One of the biggest such development projects is the vast Media Production City taking shape near Cairo, sometimes called "Hollywood on the Nile," even though it is located in the desert. Its scale can be gauged from the $550 million worth of construction work yet to be completed before 2001. On a good day there may be 2,000 people employed in the studios and other non-construction jobs on site. The project's managers, wary of being saddled with obsolete technology, have included clauses in their contract with Sony ensuring that all equipment be state-of-the-art. [3] Yet when it comes to the content of films shot at Media Production City, the Egyptian Radio and Television Union's 50 percent stake in the venture gives it ultimate editorial control.

Faced with the challenge of filling thousands of hours of airtime, television executives have limited options. Programming costs have traditionally been less prohibitive for state-sponsored broadcasters with a purely political *raison d'etre*. State revenues are drying up, however, while media competition dictates an increasingly hard-nosed commercial approach. The combination of these economic factors militates against the commissioning of challenging documentaries or innovative dramas, and means that broadcasters will instead rely on ready-made material or imports. Mexican soap operas have proved popular throughout the region. ART has bought up large quantities of old Egyptian films, and Orbit relies on programming supplied by Rupert Murdoch's Star TV.

Although advertising revenue might be expected to fill the gap, in the Middle East advertising remains woefully underdeveloped. Advertisers acknowledged the importance of satellite television by increasing their allocations to this medium to $200 million in 1997, which was almost double the figure for 1996 and roughly two thirds of 1997 spending on terrestrial television. [4] Yet future growth is not assured. Upon leaving office last year, the outgoing managing director of MBC, Hala Omran, said that she wished more local companies would learn to advertise since this in turn would fund media expansion. [5] If these companies are to take the plunge, however, they will require more reliable viewing figures than are currently available.

Not only are ratings in most countries compiled by unsophisticated methods, leaving analysts skeptical about their accuracy, but potential advertisers are increasingly unsure how best to target viewers because of the effects of the digital revolution. Digital technology allows satellites to transmit scores of channels where previously they could transmit only a few. Nilesat 101, launched by Egypt in April 1998, can handle over 80 television channels. The new generation of Arabsat satellites, the first of which was due for launching in early 1999, will provide even more capacity. With countless separate thematic channels for news, sport and drama alongside the numerous general interest channels, audience shares could become so fragmented that viewing preferences will be almost impossible to track.

Haves and Have-Nots

Despite the ambiguities surrounding market shares, advertisers will continue to pursue audiences, thereby helping to reverse the former situation in which broadcasters decided audiences' options. The problem comes in assessing whether, in the leap from total state control to market-driven programming, Middle East satellite television will ever function as an independent public service providing outlets for investigative journalism and a widened arena for uncensored policy debates.

Egypt's government boasts of using satellite television as a public service and as a catalyst for development, but "development" in this case constitutes a one-way information flow. Nilesat is Egypt's entry ticket into what Cairo proudly calls the "space club." Official speeches highlight the spinoff benefits, such as technology transfers to local scientists and technicians, and the use of Nilesat channels for educational programming and public service programs on health.

For Egyptian families hoping to tune in to Nilesat channels for lessons, however, the minimum outlay for a digital receiver geared to free-to-air transmission is 1,600 pounds ($475). Hire purchase arrangements are in hand to put the receivers within reach of ordinary people and the sales pitch is that lessons by satellite will eventually lessen the expenses of private tuition. In theory this should be attractive for parents who currently pay vast sums for after-school lessons in virtually every subject. Yet in practice, there is less demand for satellite viewing in Egypt than in other parts of the Middle East. Satellite penetration in Egypt remains under 10 percent, compared with levels of 15 to 30 percent in neighboring countries and 50 percent in parts of the Gulf. [6] Hence, most Egyptian families interested in taking advantage of Nilesat will probably still need to buy a satellite dish as well as a receiver.

Since other countries within the Nilesat footprint can also benefit from its educational service, Egypt may find itself—not for the first time—subsidizing regional development. The satellite project has already cost $160 million, which will take eight years to recoup on the basis of arrangements for leasing current spare capacity. Nilesat 101 has 12 transponders, of which seven are let to foreign broadcasters, [7] each at the rate of $3 million per year. Nilesat 102, due to be launched later this year at a further cost of $140 million, will have another 12.

Advertisers' biases toward wealthy Gulf audiences must also be taken into account, especially for Egyptian and Lebanese satellite companies, whose managers are keenly aware that, in order to maximize revenues, their programs should be suitable for Gulf consumption. Sana Mansour, head of the Egyptian Space Channel, maintains that whereas terrestrial television should be attending to local issues, satellite television needs a wider focus, "Terrestrial channels can behave like an employee, complaining about things like broken pipes, but the satellite channels have to be ambassadors for Egypt." [8] Nadim Munla, chairman of Future TV, feels that his station should promote Lebanon to Gulf investors, stressing that "life is back" in Lebanon. [9] "Life" in this context means fun and entertainment, not probing interviews with Lebanese politicians. For much of 1998, Hariri's cabinet barred Lebanon's satellite channels from covering local news.

Some claim that Arab satellite channels are contributing to a renewed sense of pan-Arabness, as people all over the Arab world tune into the same programs at the same time. Broadcast executives have recognized this potential by featuring photogenic pan-Arab extravaganzas, such as sporting events, Orbit's annual song festival, and the "edu-tainment" quiz shows offered by Future TV and MBC. Examining the rise of the press and nationalism in Europe, Benedict Anderson has argued that print-capitalism created the possibility of an "imagined community," in which individuals felt themselves to be intimately connected to millions of people they had never met. [10] Arabic-language television transcending national borders could have a comparable effect.

In deliberately reaching out to expatriate Arabs in Europe and the Americas, Arab satellite channels may also be helping to preserve ties between emigrant communities and their countries of origin. Research suggests, unsurprisingly, that first generation emigrants watch far more Arabic-language television than their offspring. [11] Nevertheless, emigrants have traditionally been a source of funds, innovation and technical expertise for the region, so anything that keeps these contacts alive could well affect future developments in the Middle East.

In the immediate future, however, prospects for uncensored news and current affairs programs on the Arab satellite channels are mixed. Neither ART nor Orbit carries any Arabic news, and Orbit has not replaced the BBC Arabic news service it axed in 1996. MBC steers clear of investigating Saudi or other contentious issues and plans in its new streamlined phase [12] to focus on entertainment rather than news. MBC executives decided early in 1998 not to pursue plans for an all-news channel. The Egyptian state's news output, whether on the Egyptian Space Channel or the Nilesat thematic channels, is unlikely to make waves, while the Syrian-owned Arab News Network, although committed to news and current affairs programming, has yet to establish itself as a strong contender in the field.

As satellite programming blends in with the overall Middle East media environment, the best barometer of a changing climate for news coverage and debate—one that is more conducive to development in the region—is probably Al Jazeera. As the end of the century approaches, the arrow on the barometer could still swing either way.

Endnotes

[1] London is home to Saudi-owned MBC, Kurdish-owned MED TV and Arab News Network, owned by Syrian President Asad's nephew. The Saudi-owned pay-TV operator, Orbit, is based in Rome.

[2] Al Jazeera has caused controversy by, among other things, leading news bulletins with coverage of the illness of King Fahd.

[3] Factual information on Media Production City was gathered during a visit on September 6, 1998. The number of permanent employees is approximately 350.

[4] According to the Pan-Arab Research Center, data quoted in *ArabAd* (February 1998), pp. 24-26.

[5] Interview with Chris Forrester in *Gulf Marketing Review* (May 1998), p. 27.

[6] Figures collated from various sources, including PARC, Eutelsat, Stat-IPSOS, and Fortune Promoseven.

[7] Four transponders are taken by the Egyptian Radio and Television Union and the ministries of education, higher education and health. A fifth is reserved for ad hoc purposes. ART and Showtime have two each. Iraq and Libya have one each. Oman, Bahrain, Ajman and the Palestinian Authority have slots on the twelfth.

[8] Interview with Sana Mansour, Cairo, August 15, 1998.

[9] Interview with Nadim Munla, Beirut, March 26, 1998.

[10] Benedict Anderson, *Imagined Communities* (London: Verso, 1991), p. 46.

[11] E.g., the study by Alec Hargreaves and Dalila Mahdjoub on families of Maghrebi origin in France, in *European Journal of Communication* 12/4 (December 1997).

[12] MBC dismissed 120 staff members during the summer of 1998.]

| "*As more and more individuals began to use internet, the resistance against blocking and filtering practices also increases.*"

Censoring Information on the Internet Has Harmful Effects on a Society

Haiping Zheng

In the following viewpoint, Haiping Zheng discusses the much-criticized Internet censorship in China and its effect on Internet users in the country. China has some of the most sophisticated technology in the world, which is dedicated to censoring and filtering "illegal" content on the Internet. But these systems do not foresee all sensitive words and are often still easily circumvented. Internet service providers are also encouraged to self-censor so that they can avoid threats of punishment from the Chinese government. Additionally, the author discusses the Chinese government's attempts to control how people access the Internet at Internet cafes. Haiping Zheng teaches at the Renmin University of China School of Law in Beijing.

"Regulating the Internet: China's Law and Practice," by Haiping Zheng, SciRes, March 2013. Reprinted by permission.

As you read, consider the following questions:

1. How many Internet users did China have by 2008?
2. What is one example of a hard-to-control website that the Chinese government blocks?
3. What is the real function of the Internet cartoon characters introduced by the city of Shenzhen, according to the viewpoint?

Introduction

China's internet censorship has drawn much international criticism. For example, in 2006, the Reporters without Board included China as one of the 13 "enemies of the Internet" (Reporters without Borders, 2006). Then in 2010, Google decided to withdraw from Chinese market, claiming that Chinese government's attempts to limit free speech on the web, combined with other factors, had led the corporation to make such a decision (Official Google Blog, 2010).

On the other hand, the picture is not that gloomy. By 2008, the number of internet users in China has reached 220 million, making China the nation with the largest number of internet users. Furthermore, due to the very nature of internet, it is often difficult for the government to control the information transmitted through internet. Despite Chinese government's efforts to censor the internet, it is doubtful how much success it can achieve.

This paper examines China's internet censorship and its effects. Part 1 provides a general introduction to the development of internet in China. Such background information is necessary for the understanding and analysis of internet censorship in China. Part 2 introduces some of the regulations that have a direct impact on internet speech. Part 3 describes some specific measures (or techniques) the Chinese government utilizes to control the internet: filtering and blocking, imposing liabilities on private parties, access control, internet "police", and "guiding" public opinion. The final part is the conclusion of the paper.

Development of Internet in China

Although China began to be connected to the internet as early as 1987, internet was not commercially available in China until 1995. From then on, internet has been growing tremendously over the years. By 2008, infrastructure has extended broadband Internet access to 92 percent of townships (Zhao, 2008).

Like many other areas of China's economic development since 1978, development of internet was largely driven by the government. As a result, China's internet hardware infrastructure is highly centralized. Currently, there exist nine state-licensed Internet Access Providers (IAPs), each of which has at least one connection to a foreign Internet backbone. All the IAPs are required to be "at least fifty-one percent controlled by State-owned companies". These IAPs, in turn, grant regional Internet Service Providers (ISPs) access to backbone connections. All these entities (IAPs and ISPs) are required to register with the designated government agents. Those who fail to comply with the regulations face the threat of being shut down (ONI, 2005).

The government's monopolistic position in internet infrastructure facilitates censorship. Because all Internet traffic passes through the nine IAPs, the government can censor the information flow by adding filtering system "at the gateways." Moreover, as Part 3 will show, the government requires ICPs and ISPs to filter internet content, resulting in severe self-censorship.

International companies have been playing a significant role in the development and maintenance of China's internet infrastructure. The Cisco system, in particular, has been integral to China's Internet development. It specifically implemented the backbone networks for at least three of China's nine IAPs. Western corporations' such "conspiring" activities have been subjected to the criticism of human rights activists (Newbold, 2003).

Chinese Government's Attempts to Control the Internet: An Overview

Before the introduction of internet, the Chinese government, under the leadership of the Chinese Communist Party (CCP), essentially controlled all the traditional mass media, including newspapers, magazines, television, radio, etc. Unsurprisingly, the government sought to control the new media even before internet became commercially available. Over the years, the government promulgated numerous regulations to control the internet. This part provides an overview of the regulations that have a direct impact on internet speech.

On February 1, 1996, China's State Council promulgated the Interim Provisions Governing Management of Computer Information Networks. It prohibits four categories of information from being produced or transmitted online: information that would harm national security, disclose state secrets, threaten social stability or promote sexually suggestive material (art. 13).

On September 20, 2000, the State Council issued the Measures for Managing Internet Information Services (Measures, 2000), which significantly extended the scope of prohibited contents. Article 15 of the 2000 Measures provides:

> ISPs (internet service providers) shall not produce, reproduce, release, or disseminate information that contains any of the following: 1) Information that goes against the basic principles set in the Constitution; 2) Information that endangers national security, divulges state secrets, subverts the government, or undermines national unity; 3) Information that is detrimental to the honor and interests of the state... 6) Information that disseminates rumors, disturbs social order, or undermines social stability... or 9) Other information prohibited by the law or administrative regulations.

It is easy to see that provisions like this are "vague, confusing and inconsistent" (Li, 2004). Yet similar provisions are present in many other internet regulations. Indeed, these provisions are so common that many Chinese seem to have "accepted" them. Few people attempted to challenge the legitimacy (or constitutionality) of such provisions. Obviously, such vague provisions can deter individual citizens from spreading "sensitive" information that may fall into one of the prohibited categories.

Internet Censorship and Its Resistance

This Part introduces some specific measures (or techniques) that China uses to control the internet. Although these measures in fact overlap with one another, for purpose of clarity, they are to be discussed separately here.

Blocking and Filtering Systems

The Chinese government consistently blocks the entire domain of certain websites that are hard to control, including some international news sources (i.e., BBC-Chinese), internal blogger servicer providers (i.e., facebook, blogger), and some other websites that often post criticism on China's human rights and social justice records (i.e., Amnesty International, Human Rights Watch, etc.) These websites are blocked regardless of their specific contents, partly because the ISPs of these websites are unlikely to "cooperate" with the Chinese government in censoring the internet content (ONI, 2005).

The general trend, though, seems to be that the Chinese government tries to filter specific "sensitive" contents rather than blocking the entire websites at the backbone level. For example, before the 2008 Olympic Games, the New York Times website was entirely blocked. During the Olympic Games, the site was partially "unblocked", rendering some URLs (Uniform Resource Locates) accessible while others inaccessible. Thus, the accessibility of a website does not guarantee that all the contents on that site will be available. Typically, the blocked contents are those that are deemed to be "sensitive" by the government. The specific "sensitive" contents change over time. However, certain contents are regularly filtered: for example, the Tiananmen Square protests of 1989, the independence of Tibet, Xinjiang and Taiwan, and the Falun Gong movement, etc. (Zittrain & Edelman, 2003; ONI, 2005).

With respect to filtering technology, China's technology is "the most sophisticated effort of its kind in the world". (ONI, 2005) As early as 1998, the Chinese government began to invest in the notorious Gold Shield software project. The main function of the Gold Shield software is to censor "illegal" contents. It can pick the sensitive words and block the relevant content. However, the effectiveness of filtering technology is unclear. The filtering systems can not foresee all the sensitive words. In addition, sophisticated internet users can often access blocked contents through various circumvention technologies.

Moreover, in recent years, as more and more individuals began to use internet, the resistance against such blocking and filtering practices also increases. The controversy over the "Green Dam Youth Escort" ("Green Dam" hereafter) provides a revealing example. The "Green Dam" software was a filtering device that was supposed to be very powerful in filtering internet contents. In May 2008, the Minister of Industry and Information (MII) spent more than 41 million yuan (about 6 million US dollars) to purchase the "Green Dam" software from two companies that had "cooperated" with Chinese government in the past. The MII then offered the software to internet users for free downloads. However, few individuals bothered to install the "free" software (Chao, 2009).

On May 19, 2009, the MII went further by sending a notification to computer manufacturers of its intention to require all new personal computers sold in China after July 1 to pre-install the "Green Dam" software. However, soon after the notification was released, there was a surge of online criticism. At the night of June 30, just several hours before the requirement was to become effective, MII issued a notice, declaring that the requirement to install the "Green Dam" software was to be postponed. [Today], the MII has not re-set the requirement for compulsory pre-installation of the software.

Controlling the ISPs and the Resulting Self-Censorship

As mentioned in Part 2, several regulations impose liabilities on ISPs, blog service providers (BSPs), and BBS (Bulletin Board System) providers, etc. For example, the 2000 Measures requires IAPs and ISPs to record the dates and times when subscribers accessed the Internet, the subscriber's account number, the addresses of all websites visited, and the telephone number used to access the Internet. The ISPs and IAPs must keep a record of this information for sixty days and provide it to the authorities upon request. Similar liabilities were imposed on BBS providers in another regulation promulgated in 2000.

Indeed, the Chinese authorities took specific actions to implement these regulations. For example, on January 9, 2009, Niubo, a blog service provider, was shut down because it transmitted "harmful information on political and current affairs" (Wu, 2009). Specifically, the closure was linked to its status as being the leading domestic circulator Charter 08, a proposal by Chinese intellectuals to reform China's politics (Garnaut, 2009).

Because of the threat of punishment, private entities (including IAPs, ISPs and BSPs) often resort to self-censorship. The following are some of the typical methods that are used by these entities to "censor" the internet. First, like the government, the private entities also resort to the filtering technology. Some forum operators have developed their own systems to catch sensitive words so that they can review the message before it is posted. As a result, when an internet user attempts to post an entry which contains a "sensitive" word, he or she would receive an immediate notice stating "this message can not be posted because it contains improper content".

Second, these private entities also employ individuals to manually delete or conceal "sensitive" posts or comments. These individuals are commonly known as "internet administrators". Their routine job is to spot and delete (or conceal) posts or comments that are deemed to be "improper". To help these internet administrators identify "improper" or "sensitive" contents, many websites encourage individuals internet users to report such contents to the administrator by clicking certain icon.

Finally, if a blog or specific forum becomes too "sensitive", the ISP (or BSP) may delete or block the blog or forum. Thus, Sina.com, China's most popular BSP, shut down numerous blogs that are too "sensitive". Even some international corporations have yielded to the pressure. For example, in December 2005, Microsoft Corporation deleted the site of a Beijing blogger from its MSN Spaces service (Barboza & Zeller, 2006). This case drew much international attention partly because it involves Microsoft, a US-based corporation. It would not have gained much attention had it been a Chinese corporation.

Like government censorship, "private censorship" is increasingly being challenged by internet users. In recent years, there had been several well-known law suits in which the owner of the shut-down blogs sued the BSPs. For example, in August 2007, Liu Xiaoyuan, a lawyer in Beijing, sued Sohu.com for deleting his blog posts. He alleged that Sohu breached the blog service contract by concealing nine articles he posted on his blog. These articles, he alleged, were "neither illegal nor obscene." Although Lawyer Liu was able to file the lawsuit in a Beijing court, he soon received a court order stating that the court would not accept the case. Liu sought to appeal. But the appellate court refused to review the case (Tang, 2007).

While the plaintiffs in most of the cases, like Mr. Liu, were unable to get their cases filed in the court, Hu Xingdou turns out to be an exception. Mr. Hu is a professor at Beijing Technology University. He had a personal website on which he posted his own articles, most of which were political comments. He paid certain fees to Beijing Xinwang Corporation, a ISP which provided the technological support for his website. However, in March 2007, Mr. Hu received a notification from Xinwang, informing him that his website was shut down because it contained "illegal information". Mr. Hu then filed a suit in a Beijing court, alleging that Xinwang breached the blog service contract. More than twenty intellectuals in Beijing, including some prominent law professors and lawyers, signed a "public letter" to support Mr. Hu. Partly because of the media pressure, the court ruled in favor of Mr. Hu, stating that Xinwang did not provide any evidence regarding what was "illegal" on Mr. Hu's website.

Mr. Hu's victory was rather exceptional. According to Mr. Hu, he knew it would be impossible to win if he alleges that the ISP infringed his right to "freedom of speech". As a tactical choice, he only alleged that ISP breached the blog service contract. Also, he only asked for a refund of the fees, not the restoration of the website. As such, the court was able to render a decision without deciding whether Mr. Hu's free speech right has been abridged.

Access Control

Currently, Chinese internet users access the internet through three major channels: personal computers, mobile phones and internet cafes. The internet cafes are the main access location for about half of Chinese internet users (CINIC, 2009).

The Chinese government sought to control each of the three accesses. The first two accesses are relatively easy to control. An individual accessing the internet through a personal computer, whether at home or at office, can be easily located. Similarly, the mobile phone owners who accessed internet could be easily identified. The following part focuses on the Chinese government's attempts to control citizens' activities in internet cafes.

The government's control is implemented mainly through two layers of registration requirement. First, every internet cafe is required to register at a designated local governmental agency. Because local governments typically limit the number of the internet cafes in a particular locality, the registration process essentially involves governmental licensing. The government would only grants the license to internet cafes that meet certain requirements. The license may be revoked if the internet cafe does not follow the "rules". For example, between June and September

2002, the government shut down 150,000 unlicensed Internet cafes (Hermida, 2002). Till day, police routinely "raids" internet cafes to see whether there is any "illegal" activity going on.

The second layer of the access control occurs at the level of individual internet users. Internet cafes are required to record every user's identity and online activities. Each cafe is required to keep these records (or "logs") for at least sixty days and to provide the records to police upon request. Currently, these rules are strictly enforced. Thus, one who does not take his valid identification card with him may not access internet in internet cafes.

Finally, all cafes are required to install monitoring software approved by the police. Such software not only monitors online activities of internet users in the cafe, but also filters certain "sensitive" information.

Criminal and Administrative Punishment

A lot of individuals have been punished for "illegal" online activities such as posting prohibited contents. In 2008 alone, it was reported that China imprisoned at least forty-nine individuals for online activities, including several individuals serving their second period of detention for internet-related crimes (Reporters without Borders, 2009; China Human Rights Defenders, 2009). For example, Liu Shaokun, a school teacher, was sentenced to one year reeducation-through-labor for posting pictures of school buildings that collapsed in the 2008 Sichuan earthquake (Human Rights in China Press Release, 2008).

Individuals may even be punished for sending private e-mails that contain "sensitive" contents. For example, in 2005, Shi Tao, a Chinese citizen, was sentenced to ten years in prison for e-mailing a "state secret" to a New York website editor. The "top secret" reportedly expressed the Party's concern about the possibility of demonstrations occurring on the fifteenth anniversary of the Tiananmen Square protest. Shi used a Yahoo e-mail to send the information. The case drew international attention partly because Yahoo "cooperated" with the Chinese government by providing information linking the e-mail to the IP address of Shi's computer (Kerstetter, 2005).

In recent years, as the internet becomes to be used by more and more individuals, the resistance against government abuse is also growing. For example, in February 2009, Wang Shuai, while working in Shanghai, posted a blog entry stating that officials in his hometown, Lingbao City in Henan province, had misappropriated funds for combating drought. To the surprise of Mr. Wang, police from Lingbao arrested him in Shanghai. Fortunately for Mr. Wang, a report in China Youth Daily (a newspaper) sparked a heated online discussion. Finally, the media pressure became so great that the high Party officials in Henan province issued an apology, compensated Wang for his eight-day detention, fired the local Party secretary, and punished three officials who misappropriated funds (Chen, 2009).

Internet Police
In January 2006, the city of Shenzhen introduced two cartoon characters that appear on all websites or internet forums in Shenzhen. The cartoons move interactively with the internet users as they navigate through web pages. In addition to linking the users to information about internet regulations and internet-crime cases, the cartoons also connect users to internet police through an Instant Messaging service for the purpose of answering users' questions about internet security. However, as officials of Shenzhen Public Security Bureau informed the reporters, the "main function" of the cartoons is "to intimidate, not to answer questions" (Qiang, 2006).

The intimidation function seems to work. It was reported that between January and May 2006, the frequency of posting "hazardous information" decreased by sixty percent, and more than 1600 Internet crime allegations were reported through the cartoon police. Thereafter, the cartoon police were introduced in many other cities (Xinhua News Agency, 2006).

"Guiding" the Public Opinion

Partially in response to the uncontrollable nature of internet, the Chinese government attempted to "guide" public opinion by hiring "internet commentators." In 2008, a report estimated that China employed more than 280,000 "internet commentators" nationwide (Bandurski, 2008). While the government never explicitly spelled out the qualifications and functions of the "internet commentators", media reports suggest that they mainly perform two tasks: first, "guiding" the internet users towards "correct" political direction; second, identifying, and sometimes deleting "harmful" information.

The "internet commentators" originated at Nanjing university in 2005: the university recruited students with school funds to advocate the "correct" line on an online student forum. The practice soon became popular at different levels of government and other Party-controlled organizations. For example, Gansu province, a largely poverty-stricken province in Northwestern China, announced to recruit 650 "internet commentators" in 2009.

Besides, the Minister of Culture developed Internet commentator trainings. Those who went though the training would receive a job certification, which would qualify them to serve as "internet commentators". There seems to be plenty of job opportunities for these 'internet commentators": not only government hire "internet commentators", major websites are required to recruit in-house teams of the government-trained commentators.

Conclusion

While censoring the internet may have some beneficial effects from the government's perspective, it does more harm than good. There are at least four reasons to conclude that governments should not censor internet.

First, although censorship might keep "bad news" from being released to the public in the short run, it can rarely do so in the long run. In today's world, although censorship may make it more difficult for individuals to find certain "sensitive" information, it can not entirely block such information. For example, many individuals in China can actually use circumvention technology to access "sensitive" information.

Second, even assume that the government can "successfully" keep certain information from being transmitted to individual citizens, such a "success" is not necessarily good. Public decisions based on one-sided information are often problematic, and may sometimes lead to disastrous consequences.

Third, such censorship may destroy citizens' trust for the government. Individuals tend to suspect the news released by government. They may think that such news has been manipulated by the government. Such a situation could be devastating for the government in the long run.

Finally, the financial costs of such censorship are huge. The Chinese government has spent a lot of money on purchasing or developing the filtering software, hiring the "internet administrators" and "internet commentators", and implementing the censorship mechanism. It is hardly possible for a democratic government to spend so much money to curtail citizens' speech.

References

Bandurski, D. (2008). China's guerrilla war for the web, far eastern economic review. URL (last checked 16 November 2012). http://www.feer.com/essays/2008/august/chinas-guerrilla-war-for-the -web

Barboza, D., & Zeller, T. (2006), Microsoft shuts blog's site after com- plaints in Beijing. NY Times. http://www.nytimes.com/2006/01/06/technology/06blog.html?_r=1& oref=slogin

Chao, L. (2009). China squeezes PC makers. Wall Street Journal. http://online.wsj.com/article/SB124440211524192081.html

Chen, J. (2009). Officials punished over land scandal. Shanghai Daily, 29 April 2009.

China Human Rights Defenders (2009). Tug of war over China's cyberspace: A sequel to journey to the heart of censorship. URL (last checked 9 March 2012). http://crdnet.org/Article/Class9/Class11/200903/20090319000543_1 4370.html

CINIC (China Internet Network Information Center) (2009). Twenty- third statistical survey report on the internet development in China. 23 March 2009.

Hermida, A. (2002). Behind China's internet red firewall URL (last checked 15 November 2012). http://news.bbc.co.uk/1/hi/technology/2234154.stm

Human Rights in China Press Release (2008). Family visits still denied to Sichuan school teacher punished after quake-zone visit. URL (last checked 29 July 2008). http://www.hrichina.org/public/contents/press?revision_Id=66556&it em_Id=6652

Kerstetter, J. (2005). Group says Yahoo helped jail Chinese journalist. CNET NEWS.COM, 6 September 2005.

Li, C. (2004). Internet content control in China. International Journal of Communications Law and Policy, 1, 5

Newbold, J. R. (2003). Aiding the enemy: Imposing liability on US corporations for selling China internet tools to restrict human rights. University of Illinois Journal of Law, Technology & Policy.

Official Google Blog (2010). A new approach to China. URL (last checked 16 November 2012). http://googleblog.blogspot.com/2010/01/new-approach-to-china.html

ONI (2005). Internet filtering in China in 2004-2005: A country study. URL (last checked 15 November 2012). http://opennet.net/sites/opennet.net/files/ONI_China_Country_Study.pdf

Qiang, X. (2006). Image of internet police: Jingjing and Chacha Online-Hong Yan. URL (last checked 17 November 2012). http://www.chinadigitaltimes.net/2006/01/image_of_internet_police_ jingjing_and_chacha_online_hon.php

Reporters without Borders (2006). List of the 13 internet enemies. URL (last checked 16 November 2012). http://www.rsf.org/List-of-the-13-Internet-enemies.html

Reporters without Borders (2009). 2009 Annual report: China. URL (last checked 16 November 2012). http://www.rsf.org/enrapport57-China.html

State Council of China (2000). Measures for managing internet information services. URL (last checked 15 November 2012). http://www.lehmanlaw.com/resource-centre/laws-and-regulations/inf ormation-technology/measures-for-managing-internet-information-ser- vices-2000.html.

Tang, X. (2007). Why delete my blog articles? Chongqing Fazhi Ribao, 29 October 2007. URL (last checked 15 November 2012). http://blog.sina.com.cn/s/blog_3eba51c501000b7l.html

Wu, V. (2009). Popular blog service provider shut down. South China Morning Post, 10 January 2009.

Xinhua News Agency (2006). Cyber police in Shenzhen to curb on-line crimes. 15 May 2006. URL (last checked 15 November 2012). http://news.xinhuanet.com/english/2006-05/15/content_4547731.htm

Zhao, Z. G. (2008). Development and administration of internet in China. URL (last checked 15 November 2012). http://www.china.org.cn/china/internetForum/2008-11/06/content_16 719106.htm

Zittrain, J., & Edelman, B. (2003). Empirical analysis of internet filtering in China. URL (last checked 15 November 2012). http://cyber.law.harvard.edu/filtering/china/

Periodical and Internet Sources Bibliography

The following articles have been selected to supplement the diverse views presented in this chapter.

David Bandurski, "China's Guerilla War for the Web," China Media Project, July 7, 2008. http://cmp.hku.hk/2008/07/07/feer-chinas-guerrilla-war-for-the-web/.

Dana Bazelon, Yung Jung Choi, and Jason F. Conaty, "Computer Crimes," *American Criminal Law Review*, 2006. https://litigation-essentials.lexisnexis.com/ webcd/app?action=DocumentDisplay&crawlid=1&doctype=cite&docid=43+Am.+Crim.+L.+Rev.+259&srctype=smi&srcid=3B15&key=a79f550cb36c5345f03d04684ed99a0c.

Nina Iacono Brown, "Should Social Networks Be Held Liable for Terrorism?," Slate, June 16, 2017. http://www.slate.com/articles/technology/future_tense/2017/06/a_new_legal_theory_for_holding_social_networks_liable_for_terrorism.html.

James J.F. Forest, "Countering Terrorism and Insurgency in the 21st Century: International Perspectives," Teaching Terror, 2007. http://www.teachingterror.net/CT21/.

Marc D. Goodman and Susan W. Brenner, "The Emerging Consensus on Criminal Conduct in Cyberspace," Internet Society of New Zealand, February 9, 2001. https://archive.org/stream/TheEmergingConsensusOnCriminalConductInCyberspace/TheEmergingConsensusOnCriminalConductInCyberspace_djvu.txt.

Internet World Stats, "Internet Usage in the Middle East," Internet World Stats, 2017. http://www.internetworldstats.com/stats5.htm.

Andrew K. Woods, "These Revolutions Are Not All Twitter," *New York Times*, February 1, 2011. http://www.nytimes.com/2011/02/02/opinion/02iht-edwoods02.html.

Jennifer Preston, "Movement Began with Outrage and a Facebook Page That Gave It an Outlet," *New York Times*, February 5, 2011. http://www.nytimes.com/2011/02/06/world/middleeast/06face.html.

CHAPTER 4

Is It Advantageous to Utilize Alternative Media?

Chapter Preface

In countries that traditionally rely on mainstream media, the question of whether it's advantageous—or moral—to utilize alternative media has been a growing question in recent years. When traditional media refuses to provide coverage for topics that consumers are interested in, they have no choice but to turn to new and alternative forms of media. The disparity between what mainstream media thinks its consumers want, compared to what they actually want, continues to grow.

Among the younger set, Americans are growing more and more passionate in expressing their views. But, conversely, free speech on college campuses is being challenged in different ways by both conservatives and progressives. Some students have protested the right of universities to invite controversial right-wing speakers who might preach hate speech, while others believe that they are *protecting* free speech by allowing such discourse.

With the shortening of the attention spans of media consumers since the advent of websites like Twitter and the current obsession with "political correctness," there are questions about the future of the free and open discourse currently found online. A way to overcome this is for media consumers to seek out news that does not cater to one specific political ideal over another. This allows for a fair and educated discourse that is not currently found within the mainstream media. Too often corporations within the mainstream media cater to one extreme ideological viewpoint—some that allow the spread of certain citizens' fascist views—without giving fair coverage to alternative perspectives.

While many mainstream media outlets are unwilling to provide nuanced coverage, there is a growing sect of mainstream media that is: satirical news. Shows like *The Daily Show*, *Last Week Tonight*, and *Full Frontal with Samantha Bee* once would have been called "fake news," but now serve to represent a new perspective, especially political, to younger voters and consumers. These shows attempt to educate media consumers while also entertaining them. This satirical viewpoint has grown to the point where it is one of the best places to educate an electorate, making those who learn from traditional sources like Fox News, CNN, ABC, or MSNBC less informed or even completely misinformed.

> *"Americans are turning increasingly away from papers and TV, and towards web-based sources."*

New Media Is Broadening Its Scope

Denise Robbins

In the following viewpoint, Denise Robbins discusses the connection between alternative media and climate change coverage. As media consumers increasingly turn to web-based news, "new media" has begun to expand its reporting. In 2014, the website Upworthy released the findings of a poll of its readers on the topics they wanted more coverage on, and the number one answer was climate change and clean energy. Since then, multiple new media entities have taken great strides to provide coverage of what is socially considered a "critically important issue." Robbins is communications director at Chesapeake Climate Action Network.

As you read, consider the following questions:

1. Who is now providing more coverage of climate change?
2. Why is it important to have experts to report on subjects such as climate change?
3. Why might the hiring of Roger Pielke Jr. ruffle feathers?

"This New Media Trend Will Leave You Optimistic About the Future," by Denise Robbins, Media Matters for America, March 18, 2014. Reprinted by permission.

A s climate change coverage has been suffering in mainstream media, alternative, web-based media sources are starting to give more attention to the issue of global warming.

On March 10, Upworthy released the findings of a poll of its readers on what topic they wanted more coverage of—the number one answer was climate change and clean energy. This is the latest in a trend of new media sources actively working to provide more coverage of global warming, in contrast to traditional media that are providing "shockingly little" coverage to a "critically important issue." Meanwhile, to receive their news content Americans are turning increasingly away from papers and TV, and towards web-based sources, a term collectively known as "new media."

A paper from the Yale Forum on Climate Change & Media found that web multimedia is "poised to reshape news coverage on science and climate," telling of a burgeoning opportunity for climate change stories—that "the time for new media has come":

> "[Mainstream media] has been doing things the same way for so long you can't be imaginative," says Nicholson, a New York-based science journalist. As television and the Internet merge, she sees coverage taking on forms fully adapted to the possibilities of digital production. "It's going to be fast, social and everything will be mobile," she says. "We have an opportunity to change the way we tell stories."

So how are new media turning to the topic of climate change?

Upworthy

When announcing the findings of their poll calling for more climate and clean energy coverage, Upworthy simultaneously announced that they are going to partner with Climate Nexus, a nonprofit that works to communicate the impacts of climate change, to produce more stories on the topic.

Upworthy is known for "optimizing optimism" through curating content and adding irresistible headlines that will compel readers to share their stories. Climate change is often seen through a pessimistic lens—a recent study of broadcast evening news programs found that when they did cover the issue, they often decoupled messages about the threat of climate change from messages about what can be done. Previous studies have suggested that when a message conveys a threat but not a potential action to address it, such as turning to clean energy to mitigate global warming, the message may be rejected.

One video summarizes the difference with Upworthy's approach: it starts with traditional news coverage describing the threat of climate change, and then describes what one community is doing to transition to clean energy while battling a powerful coal company.

Think the public isn't interested in climate change? The video has 102,000 Facebook likes (more than its already high average).

Mashable

On January 28, social media news website *Mashable* announced that it would hire Andrew Freedman as its first writer for its new "climate desk," to write about "extreme weather as well as the science behind it," according to Mashable's executive editor Jim Roberts. Freedman was named as the second-most "prolific" climate change writer of 2013 by the Daily Climate.

Since the announcement, Freedman has published many compelling articles on extreme, sometimes fascinating weather events, including a look at how Greenland ice melt is going to affect sea level rise, and a snow-free Iditarod Trail Sled Dog Race. Freedman also writes about political actions designed to bring attention to and address climate change. In an interview with MashableHQ, Freedman explained why it is imperative for *Mashable* and other alternative media outlets to invest in climate change reporting:

> Weather and climate have become such a big story for so many reasons over the past several years, yet mainstream media outlets have been cutting back on specialized science reporting. For in depth climate reporting you really need to bring in reporters who have a background in climate science and weather in order

to make the information truly value-added, and it's laudable that *Mashable* is investing in this subject area. This just isn't a subject about which you can easily aggregate or curate your content and then call it a day.

Slate

In January, Eric Holthaus was hired to report on weather and climate. As Buzzfeed reported, the "internet meteorologist and social media fanatic" has had social media success with weather stories before the move to Slate:

> The rise of the internet weatherperson has been long in the making. As a platform, the internet is a perfect home for something as universal, media-rich, and consequential as weather. And the traffic metrics appear to agree. At Quartz, where Holthaus posted weather stories before his move to Slate, his weather content "was reliably two to three times more trafficked than the average post" on the site, he told BuzzFeed.

Holthaus made headlines last fall when he pledged to never again fly on an airplane, inciting a #nofly pledge. A Rolling Stone profile showed how he takes the extra step to connect weather to climate change, which "many of his colleagues refuse to do."

Slate is also home to the "Bad Astronomer" Phil Plait, who frequently writes about climate science and criticizes those who deny the connection between human activities and global warming.

FiveThirtyEight

Perhaps not all new media climate coverage will be lauded by the climate science community. FiveThirtyEight, the new "data journalism" media venture spearheaded by Nate Silver, relaunched on March 17. The site promises to cover science more than the old FiveThirtyEight, and the website recently hired Roger Pielke, Jr., a political scientist who focuses on climate change impacts and policy, as a science writer. This choice may ruffle some feathers because Pielke is most known for downplaying the connection

Free Speech in Broadcast Media

Although indecent speech is protected by the First Amendment, speech in broadcast media has been restricted because of its omnipresence and its accessibility to children. Under the Federal Communications Commission's current policy, broadcast content is indecent if it includes content about sexual or excretory activities, or if it is patently offensive given contemporary community standards. When determining if something is "patently offensive," the FCC considers how explicit or graphic the material is, the length or repetition of the material, and whether the material is intended to titillate or is presented for shock value.

For many years, the FCC primarily enforced indecency claims for broadcasters' use of the "seven dirty words" uttered in a monologue by the same name performed by comedian George Carlin. The indecency policy was generally not enforced for single utterances of these words ("fleeting expletives"). But that changed in 2004 as a result of viewers' complaints about the infamous "wardrobe malfunction" that exposed Janet Jackson's breast during the Super Bowl. The FCC first applied its current policy to a Golden Globe Awards live broadcast during which an award recipient stated "this is really, really f***ing brilliant" during his acceptance speech. The FCC reasoned that fleeting expletives can be indecent because even one utterance of these words could harm children, but expletives may be permissible if they are integral to the artistic content of the show or occur as part of a "bona fide newscast." The FCC determines what fleeting material is indecent and what qualifies as "artistic" or "news."

In the upcoming case *FCC v. Fox Television Stations*, the Supreme Court must determine if the FCC indecency enforcement policies regarding expletives and nudity violate the right to free speech granted in the First Amendment to the U.S. Constitution. Under its current policy, the FCC ruled that fleeting expletives on two live awards shows, the CBS "Early Show" and the scripted drama "NYPD Blue" were indecent. The broadcasters argue that the FCC policy is vague because it provides no clear guidelines for what is prohibited, which abridges free speech by requiring broadcasters to avoid a wide variety of content. In general, any abridgement of free speech must be clear and specific enough to prevent subjective and indiscriminate enforcement.

"Indecent Exposure: The FCC and Free Speech," by Jennifer Groscup, **American Psychological Association,** December 2011, Vol 42, No. 11.

of weather extremes to climate change, and some experts have criticized his data analysis. For instance, in his most recent testimony before Congress, every one of his "Take-Home Points" focused on certain measures of extreme weather where there has been no documented increase in the United States—even though Pielke acknowledged later in his testimony that a "considerable body of research projects that various extremes may become more frequent and/or intense in the future as a direct consequence of the human emission of carbon dioxide." However, by downplaying that research, Pielke's statements have often been used by Republicans to deny any connections between climate change and trends in certain extreme weather events.

Furthermore, climate scientist Michael Mann has previously criticized how Nate Silver handled the subject of climate change, including that he "falls victim to the fallacy that tracking year-to-year fluctuations in temperature (the noise) can tell us something about predictions of global warming trends (the signal)."

Gawker Media

On March 3, Gawker Media, parent company to LifeHacker, Gizmodo, and more, launched their new weather-focused site titled "The Vane." Dennis Mersereau, contributor to the *Washington Post*'s Capital Weather Gang, is one of the site's first writers and has previously covered the connection of certain weather extremes, such as increasingly intense Western wildfires, to climate change.

Moreover, Gizmodo—Gawker Media's design and technology blog—consistently gives considerable attention to global warming, publishing articles on the science and effects of climate change, and financial and technological responses on how to act. Gizmodo's "Biggest Science Stories of 2013" included that humans were "officially blamed for climate change."

> "In the name of emotional well-being, college students are increasingly demanding protection from words and ideas they don't like."

Free Speech Is at Risk

Jim Sleeper

In the following excerpted viewpoint, Jim Sleeper discusses the so-called free speech crusaders attempting to find an ideological foothold on college campuses. The author discusses the actions of Greg Lukianoff, the president of the Foundation for Individual Rights in Education (FIRE). Lukianoff and others claim that overprotective parenting leads to children becoming sensitive to free speech. But this commentary on "coddling" threatens liberal education because it is perpetuated by people who feel that they are unable to talk about how things "used to be," when overt racism was accepted within conservative, white male circles. Sleeper is a lecturer in political science at Yale and author of Liberal Racism and The Closest of Strangers: Liberalism and the Politics of Race *in New York.*

"What the Campus 'Free Speech' Crusade Won't Say," by Jim Sleeper, Alternet/Alternet .org, September 4, 2016. Reprinted by permission.

As you read, consider the following questions:

1. What is an example of a past "paroxysm of alarm and rage," according to the author?
2. Why and when does the author say that scapegoating works?
3. How does money relate to free speech on college campuses, according to the author?

Whenever American civil society has been under great stress, if not, indeed, falling apart, self-appointed champions of the conventional wisdom and traditional values have ginned up public paroxysms of alarm and rage at selected internal enemies to blame for the crisis.

In the 1690s, it was the witches, hysterical women and girls whom Puritans said had been taken by Satan. In the 1840s, it was Catholic immigrants, who were said by a presidential candidate to be besotted with "rum, Romanism, and rebellion." In every decade before and since then, it has been feral Negroes. In the 1920s, it was anarchists, Reds, and pushy Hebrews. In the 1950s, it was American Communist spies for Stalin, the Satan of that time. In the 1960s, it was hippies, riotous blacks and traitorous opponents of the Vietnam War. Since 2001, it has been American Muslims and, in 2003, it was critics of the Iraq War.

Now a new cohort of crusaders has found a new internal enemy: coddled, petulant college students and some of their professors, who, we're being told, are forcing university administrators to silence and punish others who exercise freedoms of inquiry and expression in ways that offend and hurt the complainers.

We're also being told that these "cry-bullies" of "political correctness" are winning such protections by perpetrating what one of their supposed, much-ballyhooed, victims, former Harvard president Lawrence Summers, calls a "creeping totalitarianism" on our nation's campuses. They're destroying the freedoms of expression and open inquiry that a liberal education should cultivate in students, not protect them against.

If this new paroxysm has a manifesto, it's "The Coddling of the American Mind," with a scarifying subtitle: "In the name of emotional well-being, college students are increasingly demanding protection from words and ideas they don't like. Here's why that's disastrous for education—and mental health."

It was written by Greg Lukianoff, president of the Foundation for Individual Rights in Education (FIRE), and Jonathan Haidt, a business psychologist at New York University and, like Lukianoff, an itinerant preacher of their jeremiad against over-protective parenting and pedagogy that, although neither man likes to say it explicitly, is "liberal" in the colloquial and pejorative sense of that term.

Literally millions of American college alumni have fallen for this account of where the threat to liberal education is coming from. The Atlantic rode the tidal wave of the 500k-plus shares that "The Coddling" yielded, following up with a videotaped conversation between Lukianoff and the magazine's then-editor James Bennet (now the New York Times' editorial-page editor); with brief accounts by Lukianoff and Haidt of how they'd come to write the essay; with an essay by Yale Child Psychologist Erika Christakis, who had become one of the FIRE's supposed martyrs, silenced by rampaging hordes of the politically correct on the altar of free speech.

The more closely I've looked at this new "enemy" of free speech on campus, the more I've been drawn—and invite you to come along with me—to look at the self-professed defenders of individual rights in education who've been warning us about this scourge. Lukianoff has been a tactically brilliant point man for a larger, conservative campus campaign of which the FIRE is decidedly a part by virtue of its funding, many of its personnel, and, most importantly, its strategy and tactics.

I've begun this examination briefly today (Sept. 3, 2016) in the New York Times, but there's only so much one can report in 900 words. So, here goes.

Lukianoff has been indefatigable, almost manic, rushing from the foundation's lavishly appointed suites on Walnut Street in Philadelphia to campuses and green rooms across the country. Piously he brandishes First Amendment arguments to portray politically correct students and the administrators who indulge them as serious threats to open inquiry and expression.

But I, on the other hand, having witnessed the discrepancy between what the FIRE chose to highlight at one of those campuses, Yale, and what was actually going on there in a huge, college-wide reckoning with race and other matters, found Lukianoff to be more a propagandist and provocateur than a tribune of individual rights in education.

How Paroxysms Work

Let me say first that the more I've looked at crusades of this kind, the more I've been struck by similarities between this one and the earlier paroxysms I've mentioned:

- Always—and no matter whether the orchestrators of public spasms against internal traitors sound their alarms impulsively and demagogically or coolly and strategically, they get tons of support from less-talented and fortunate people who are frightened, too, by a sense that their society is unravelling. Witch-hunters, lynch-mobs, McCarthyite anti-Communists, white supremacist "militia" members, and cheerleaders and apologists in the media emerge in great numbers, out of nowhere, as the paroxysms approach their peaks.

- Always, these spasms of fear and loathing grip the public precisely when the conventional wisdom is unraveling on its own account, not because of any serious damage done to it by the groups being targeted. The scapegoating works because it diverts an increasingly nervous public's attention from deeper, broader dangers that most people fear to face head-on—dangers inherent in the blunders and deceits of the conventional wisdom's own champions, who most of us have a stake in believing and following at least some of the time.

So the crusaders and their followers find an almost seductive, even thrilling relief and release in assailing the more-vulnerable targets being presented to them. Some even find the prospect of naming, sighting, and punishing the enemy so thrilling that they go right out and join the hunt for prey that can be held up plausibly as proof of the disloyalty and danger: Sacco and Vanzetti as anarchists, Julius and Ethel Rosenberg as Jewish Communist spies, Willie Horton and O.J. Simpson as feral blacks, and so on. It works in the tawdry, predictable ways that leaders of these rituals understand only too well.

- Once a public paroxysm has been exposed to sunlight and has begun to subside, many people begin to regard its chief witch-hunters, commie hunters, and prurient scourges of decadent youth as more hysterical, sinister, and destructive of their own society than their scapegoated prey ever were.

That new clarity can prompt regret and even penitence among the scapegoaters. One Sunday in 1697, seven years after the last execution of a witch in Salem, Massachusetts, Judge Samuel Sewall, who'd presided over the trials, stood silently, head bowed, in Boston's Old South Meeting House as the pastor, Samuel Willard, read aloud a note from him confessing his "guilt contracted...at Salem" and desired "to take the blame and shame of it, asking... that God...would powerfully defend him against all temptations for Sin for the future...."

Senator Joe McCarthy never asked forgiveness for brandishing his largely fictitious lists of "Communists" in government and universities and for ruining so many lives and striking terror into many others, but he fell apart under scrutiny. Defense Secretary Robert McNamara, hard-driving architect of a war in Vietnam that began with the largely fabricated Gulf of Tonkin incident and continued with fraudulent warnings of danger to the Free World, confessed tearfully in "The Fog of War" that the war was undertaken with deceit and delusion. Republican political operative Lee Atwater, whose television ads hyping feral blacks helped cost Democratic presidential candidate Michael Dukakis the 1988 election, begged forgiveness from African-Americans on his deathbed.

My reading of Greg Lukianoff, the new paroxysm's ring-master, is that he'll end up giving us a sad demonstration of the same. In the course of this essay, I'll suggest several reasons why, and why the paroxysm about political correctness is doomed.

Principles vs. Provocations

In November 2015, Lukianoff was invited to Yale by Roger Kimball, chair of the board of the William F. Buckley, Jr. Program there and a member of the board of the Sarah Scaife Foundation, one of the substantial funders of Lukianoff's FIRE. Also inviting Lukianoff to Yale that day were Professor Nicholas Christakis and his wife Erika Christakis, "free speech" crusaders who'd already hosted Lukianoff at Harvard when they'd taught there in 2013, when the FIRE named Harvard one of the ten worst colleges for free speech in America.

At Yale last November, Erika Christakis had just ignited a free-speech controversy with a public letter to students in which she criticized the university's council of cultural-center advisors for cautioning against wearing culturally offensive Halloween costumes, such as those involving wearing blackface or feathered Native American headdresses. To Christakis, this was bureaucratic overreach, but hundreds of students signed an open letter condemning her for underestimating the sensitivities of those who might be offended.

I've described this controversy at some length on AlterNet, but it's worth noting that all of these open letters affirmed everyone's rights to free expression. As Matthew Frye Jacobson, a professor of American studies, history and African-American studies at Yale, told the New York Times, the FIRE's spin, and the subsequent storm of media coverage, was "a complete misconstruction of what happened. The cultural affairs committee made its statement about

Halloween costumes, The Christakises critiqued that; the students critiqued them. Then everyone in the world criticized the students. From beginning to end, it was never a matter of [suppressing] free speech."

No one at Yale was censured or punished by any government agency or by any administrator, faculty committee or, as far as I know, any individual faculty member.

No one, at any time, demanded or even suggested that Erika Christakis stop teaching her popular course on early childhood education. At one point in the controversy, though, an angry, black-led student group, Next Yale, posted a list of demands on President Salovey's door and others who confronted Nicholas Christakis in the courtyard at midnight, among them a demand that the Christakises be dismissed as heads of one of Yale's residential colleges. That demand was echoed vituperatively by an immature student who yelled it right into Nicholas Christakis' face in an open confrontation in the residential courtyard.

Salovey promptly reaffirmed his faith in the Christakises' "deep dedication to undergraduates," and the demand that they be dismissed as heads of their residential college died. But they took leaves of absence and cancelled their spring courses as their friend Lukianoff and the FIRE constructed and dramatized a false narrative, peddled by many in the media, casting Erika Christakis as a martyr to political correctness on the altar of free speech.

I've told the truth about that narrative before at AlterNet and won't do it again in this essay. (In an address to Yale's freshmen this year, President Peter Salovey, too, assailed what he called "false narratives" about freedom of speech at Yale and other colleges, although he didn't mention any one by name.) Since then I've learned more about Lukianoff's involvement in generating such narratives, and now is the time to share and assess it, the better to help today's paroxysm wind down.

At the Buckley Program's free-speech conference, Lukianoff delighted a pre-registered audience by quipping that, to hear recent student denunciations of Erika Christakis' defense of the right to wear blackface and Native American headdresses on Halloween, "you would have thought someone wiped out an entire Indian village."

According to a student who'd registered for the conference because he was interested in freedoms of speech but had no conservative preconceptions, the tone for the audience's response had already been set by its mostly older, conservative Yale alumni members—decent, angry, somewhat clueless men whom the speakers engaged by preaching to the choir, their implicit message being that "We all know what we all know has happened to this college."

By making "what has happened" explicit, Lukianoff's quip prompted a burst of laughter that released a pent-up anger because his listeners were relieved to hear someone say what they, hemmed in by habitual decency or inhibition, had been afraid to say themselves.

But then a student who'd slipped into the audience without registering got up and demanded to know what was so funny about genocide. He put up some posters he'd been carrying around campus urging students to "stand with women of color."

As he was escorted out by security, the other student I've mentioned posted Lukianoff's remark about wiping out an Indian village on Facebook's "Overheard at Yale" page, where it was read by some Native American students meeting elsewhere on campus. They and some others converged outside the conference, shouting, "Genocide is not a joke" and brandishing signs.

Apparently eager to face them was one of the alumni in the Buckley audience, Scott C. Johnston, Yale '82, a self-described "conservative, data geek, blogger, adjunct professor, prediction-market maven." With the air of a man finding what he'd come looking for, he'd leaned over to another alumnus as the lone student protester was leaving and said, "This isn't over."

Now, as the other protesters converged outside, Johnston leaned over again and said, "They're here." Who "they" were is explained on his blog, The Naked Dollar: "Out of curiosity," he writes disingenuously (clearly, it was more than curiosity), "I went out to look. There were perhaps twenty students, in high dudgeon, trying to get in to disrupt the conference (did I mention it was about free speech?). I engaged them, which was probably silly. 'Why are you here?'

"'We are Native Americans and you are talking about burning down Native American villages.' (They looked about as Native American as Elizabeth Warren—were they appropriating a culture?)

"'You realize, right, that no one in there is advocating burning down villages, Native American or otherwise? That it was merely an analogy to describe something bad?'

"Apparently they did, but that didn't matter. We said the words, and that 'trivialized' genocide, and that was the offense. I said, 'You do realize that you don't have the right not to be offended, right?'

"How wrong I was about that, I later reflected. That may be true, Constitutionally, but I was in a 'safe space' where these delicate orchids are protected from hearing unpleasant things. The right not to be offended now always trumps the right to free speech."

Johnston's observations so far are reasonable, or at least arguable. But soon they become the conservative "free speech" campaign's oft-repeated talking points. As Johnston's ideology and rhetoric got the best of him, he began to soar:

> "Teachers are now widely afraid of their own liberal students, because the slightest slip—the absence of a trigger warning, for instance—can result in accusations of micro-aggressions, racism, sexism, cisgenderism, whateverism, and that can result in getting tossed from tenure track. The administrators who make these decisions are afraid of the students, too, because fundamentally, the left has become a mob, and mobs are dangerous. These are the bullies of our time."

Johnston wasn't soaring alone. His post went viral on conservative sites under headlines like "Regressive Liberalism," and when Lukianoff appeared on Washington, DC's Diane Rehm show, a listener posted this comment:

"Professors should tell these sensitive darlings to go pound sand if they don't like what they are hearing. What do they expect when they graduate and enter the real world of work, and find out their boss and co-workers don't give a darn about their 'feelings'? Or if they are discussing politics or sports around the coffee pot? And God forbid these babies ever read, or engage people on, this comment board. Microagressions galore! Their heads will explode!"

This is the language of white men who are nostalgic for youths they don't clearly remember—they might wince to recall some of the things they did and said at 19. Some of them may be feeling marginal in their own country and are determined to do something about it—or to have somebody else do something about it. In "The Authoritarian Personality Revisited," Peter F. Gordon recalls Theodor Adorno's and colleagues' construction of "a distinctive attitudinal structure, called 'authoritarianism,' which consisted of nine characteristics," including a "tendency to be on the lookout for, and to condemn, reject, and punish people who violate conventional values."

Whatever the merits of categorizing personalities that way (Gordon questions them), Johnston displayed that tendency energetically, and Lukianoff soon gratified it even more when he and Nicholas Christakis, with whom he was staying while visiting Yale, walked out into the courtyard of Christakis' residential college to meet a group of black and Latino students who were returning from a wrenching confrontation with Yale College Dean Jonathan Holloway.

It was then that one of the students, a roughly 20-year-old black woman, flushed with the anguish and excitement of the campus upheavals, instantiated anyone's fantasy of a "cry-bully" by hurling imprecations into Christakis's face, accusing him of failing "to create a place of comfort and home" and, in practically the same breath, shouting, "Who the f**k hired you?"

Video-cam at the ready, Lukianoff caught the outburst, which was posted quickly by Tucker Carlson's conservative "The Daily

Caller" website under a headline, "Meet the Privileged Yale Student Who Shrieked at Her Professor," with photos of her and her parents' suburban Connecticut home and a note about its $700,000-plus assessed value. Needless to say, the video went viral, bringing the student death threats that drove her to seek police protection and go into hiding.

The conservative free-speech campaign has drawn many other prurient scourges of the decadent young to prowl campuses seeking the thrill of sighting a specimen of the enemy who has become so vivid, so haunting, in their imaginations.

Chasing the specter, they can forget about the Iraq war, the 2008 financial meltdown, the mass killings, the road rage, the gladitorialization of sports, the degrading, ever-more intrusive marketing, and Donald Trump's stampede through conventional herds of sacred political cows, all of these horrors discrediting the neo-liberal paradigm within which the hunters have lived and moved and had their beings. Finally, they can find a target.

Given its First Amendment absolutism, FIRE's engagement with Yale was even more ironic, because no government official, university administrator, faculty committee, or, as far as I know, individual faculty member ever threatened or effectively chilled the Christakises' or anyone else's opportunity to speak and teach freely.

The only "threats" that the FIRE could cite—and did cite loudly and vividly enough to provoke more of them—came from the angry black students who posted their demands on Salovey's door and confronted Nicholas Christakis in the courtyard. But should it really be so hard for Lukianoff and Johnston to imagine that a young black woman undergraduate, seeing an upsurge of racist violence and racist disenfranchisement tactics off campus, might cry out for the refuge, caring, and resources to reckon with injustice that her college's own marketing promised her?

Of course, she shouldn't be coddled but challenged to reconcile her overwrought perceptions with complex realities. But if any of her critics could pause to imagine how he might feel as a white student in a 93% non-white student body, on a campus most of whose custodial and dining hall staff were white and where most street crimes near campus were committed by whites, mightn't he assess a few black students' histrionic student reactions with a little more nuance and, frankly, a little more heart?

[...]

If Lukianoff's video was meant to correct the politically correct, it had the contradictory effect of chilling the freedoms of expression that the FIRE and Scott Johnston claim to defend even in highly offensive speech. ("You do realize that you don't have the right not to be offended, right?", Johnston had said to the Native American students. And Erika Christakis, in her open letter on Halloween costumes, had asked, "Is there no room anymore for a child or young person to be a little bit obnoxious... a little bit inappropriate or provocative or, yes, offensive? American universities were once a safe space not only for maturation but also for a certain regressive, or even transgressive, experience; increasingly, it seems, they have become places of censure and prohibition.")

No, universities haven't become places of censure and prohibition, at least not before Lukianoff took out his video-cam and used his own rights to shut down someone else's, a good example of what the conservative "free speech" campaign is doing. That video and the angry Native American students were enough to make Johnston, like alumni of other colleges that have had similar demonstrations, some led by black and Latino students, decide to stop funding what they see as coddled undergraduates and weak-kneed administrators.

"This is not your daddy's liberalism," Johnston told the New York Times. "I don't think anything has damaged Yale's brand quite like that" video of the black student shouting at the professor.

A college has more than a brand. It has a mission to teach the young the arts and disciplines of open inquiry and democratic deliberation. That mission is sometimes compromised by immature students who disrupt civil discourse and violate other students' rights, even while demonstrating against racism or sexual assault. Some professors do peddle propaganda and impose orthodoxies instead of stimulating free inquiry. Some deans do "guide" social life with rules that infantilize and tribunals that short-circuit due process. The U.S. Department of Justice's Office of Civil Rights has bureaucratized such "guidance" in ways, beyond my scope here, that only make it easier to deny due process in order to advance feminist strictures. Political correctness can be dangerous if it dominates students' politically and intellectually formative experiences.

But I, too, was at Yale last fall, teaching a political science seminar on "Journalism, Liberalism, and Democracy," and although I saw "that video," little else that I saw would have damaged Yale's "brand" or liberal education's mission had it not been so badly, willfully misrepresented. Hundreds of white students had their first intimate conversations about race with classmates of color. A thousand, of all colors, joined a vibrant campus "March of Resilience." Another thousand convened in the chapel, where I saw them hear classmates and professors speak from their deepest humanity, without malevolence or duplicity. As the author of Liberal Racism and a journalist who lived among and wrote about angry black New Yorkers for years, I know gratuitous racial "theater" when I see it. I didn't see much of it at Yale.

"I was disturbed by the discrepancies between what was actually happening on campus and how it was being portrayed in the media," said one of my students, a young white man of classically "establishment" bearing. "It wasn't exactly a protest. It was a moment of education. The entire campus was confronting collective emotions and challenges in a way I'd never experienced. It was beautiful. And it needed to be emotional—so it was."

Yet what many Americans know about such "moments of education" is what they're being shown by a campaign that's peddling antipathy and an ideology that condemns earnest, even if immature, students and protective administrators but that touts "free markets" as better guarantors of individual rights. Are they?

Morals and Dollars

"Our colleges and universities, though lavishly funded and granted every perquisite which a dynamic capitalist economy can offer, have become factories for the manufacture of intellectual and moral conformity," thundered Roger Kimball, board chairman of the Yale Buckley Program, board member of the Sarah Scaife Foundation (one of the FIRE's important funders), and author of "Re-taking the University—A Battle Plan" at a black-tie dinner the Buckley Program sponsored last year in New York's Hotel Pierre.

But videotaping protesting students and putting others into tuxedos in elegant hotels can't disguise the truth that the more market-driven a college, the more anxious it is to restrict free speech. Most deans and trustees serve not politically correct pieties but pressures to satisfy student "customers" and to avoid negative publicity, liability, and losses in "brand" or "market share."

The campaign to deflect this reality began in 1951, when William F. Buckley's God and Man at Yale urged alumni to roll back professors' godless socialism. In 1953, Buckley helped found the Intercollegiate Studies Institute, which trains students to counter "liberal" betrayals of "our nation's founding principles—limited government, individual liberty, personal responsibility, the rule of law, market economy,... ideas that are rarely taught in your classroom."

Again, though, universities are among the few places where "founding principles" are discussed often and rigorously enough to show that, in practice, some principles subvert others. For example, Lukianoff speaks often and everywhere of reinvigorating "the marketplace of ideas," but ideas in a university (and a healthy democracy) emerge from a culture of open inquiry and expression based in mutual respect, not market exchange values.

"You can't build a clear conservatism out of capitalism, because capitalism disrupts culture," said Sam Tanenhaus, biographer of the American conservative icon Whittaker Chambers, now writing a biography of William F. Buckley, Jr., in a lecture in 2007 at the conservative American Enterprise Institute.

Tanenhaus' observation about the tension between today's capitalism and democratic or republican culture is anathema to the ultra-conservative Lynde and Harry Bradley Foundation, the Scaife Family foundations, the Earhart, John Templeton, Koch-Brothers' DonorsTrust (a conduit for donors for grants not made under their own names), and other foundations that sustain conservative think tanks like the AEI and a myriad of campus-targeting organizations— including FIRE, the Intercollegiate Studies Institute, The David Horowitz Freedom Center (whose "Academic Bill of Rights" would mandate more hiring of conservative faculty and would monitor professors' syllabi for "balance") and Campus Watch (which tracks and condemns liberal professors' comments on the Middle East). These organizations stoke public anger against political correctness as a threat to academic freedom and to the free market economy that they keep insisting enhances it.

Their "free speech" campaign is really a culture war and a class war carried out on several fronts by a much larger network of organizations that are also funded by the very same foundations. The phrase "right wing" is thrown around so often that I was surprised to learn just how "right-wing" the funders of the FIRE and the other groups really are.

Harry Bradley was one of the original charter members of the far right-wing John Birch Society, along with another Birch Society board member, Fred Koch, the father of Koch Industries' billionaire brothers and owners, Charles and David Koch.

Richard Mellon Scaife, progenitor of the Scaife Family foundations, attended Deerfield Academy as a boy and got thrown out of Yale after a year. He developed a passion for advancing a conservative agenda and was an avid funder of efforts to impeach Bill Clinton. He wrote a check to FIRE for $150,000 in 2013, having donated similar amounts in 2012 and 2011, according to tax documents posted on the foundation's website. (He died in 2014, but the Sarah Scaife Foundation, with

Roger Kimball on its board, continues his work, as do the other Scaife family foundations.)

The Bradley Foundation is one of the most aggressively, unapologetically racist grant-makers of any great substance in America. Not only did it help Charles Murray (with a $100,000 grant) to finish writing The Bell Curve when even conservative groups were distancing themselves from that project; in 2010 Bradley contributed $10,000 toward putting up voter suppression billboards in black neighborhoods of Milwaukee that depicted a black man behind bars above the message, "Voting Fraud is a Felony."

But, even putting politically correct sensitivities aside in deference to First Amendment rights, there is something so thoughtless and clueless—or else subliminally provocative—in Lukianoff's analogy to "wiping out an Indian village" quip and in the distribution of "that video" of the overwrought black student that one can't help but wonder if he and his funders just slip opportunistically into targeting angry non-whites because that boosts their campaign's appeal to people looking for scapegoats, or if they're conscious racists themselves. You certainly don't see many or any people of color holding any staff positions at the FIRE or in the other organizations in its network.

The foundation has won more than a million dollars from Bradley and half a million dollars from DonorsTrust, It had $7 million in revenue and $6 million in assets in June of 2015. Yet, basing its tax exemption on its commitments to addressing "censorship, freedom of speech, and press issues," it deflects liberal and leftist criticism of its agenda by fighting draconian campus speech codes and other constraints on freedoms of expression. It has even defended Israel- bashers against some colleges' efforts to silence their protests as anti-Semitic hate speech, because, as FIRE reminds us, the First Amendment protects it, at least in public universities.

Lukianoff has also gone somewhat out of his way to post appeals to "Stand Up for Global Academic Freedom," saying that it's "under threat across the world from Turkey to China to the USA." With all due respect to slippery slopes, it's more than a bit slippery to lump American university bureaucracies' encroachments on academic freedom with draconian crackdowns by governments abroad.

Ironically, FIRE has been silent lately about David Horowitz's efforts to get state legislatures to enact his "Academic Bill of Rights," which would use government power to monitor and shape academic freedom, in clear violation of the First Amendment. Yet David French, Lukianoff's predecessor as the FIRE's president, supported Horowitz's project in public testimony.

It's characteristic of Lukianoff's modus that he tells everyone he's a liberal Democrat and that he worked at the American Civil Liberties Union. Never mind that he left the ACLU to lead the FIRE, whose grants come from the tightly linked conservative foundations I've mentioned. His boards of directors and advisors include well-known conservatives such as George Will and T. Kenneth Cribb, assistant for domestic affairs to President Ronald Reagan and a former president of the Intercollegiate Studies Institute. The Yale Buckley Program's Roger Kimball is on the board of the Sarah Scaife Foundation, one of FIRE's chief funders, according to tax documents posted on the foundation's website.

> *"Computerworld reports that 75% of writers in free countries self-censor due to fears of mass surveillance."*

The Tendency to Self-Censure Limits Digital Media

SARTRE

In the following viewpoint, the writer SARTRE discusses the growing issues of free speech and independent media coverage in the electronic age. The author discusses how people's attention spans are shortening, much thanks to the brevity on websites like Twitter. Additionally, the piece notes the surge of "political correctness" in reporting and provides recommendations on where people should find news that does not have one specific political ideal over another. With reporters choosing to self-censure and the rapid expansion of digital media on the Internet, SARTRE also questions the future of a free and open discourse online. SARTRE is the pen name of James Hall, a reformed, former political operative.

"Alternative Media Future and Risk," by SARTRE, BATR, January 27, 2015. Reprinted by permission.

As you read, consider the following questions:

1. Why does the mainstream media consider "alternative media" as negative?

2. What percentage of writers in free countries self-censor due to fears of mass surveillance, according to the viewpoint?

3. What is the importance of allowing independent inquiry or social criticism online?

The seemingly futile plight of Western Civilization can best be explained that the inhabitants of European heritage are vastly unaware of their own history and have adopted an apathetic attitude to their own survival self-interest. The horrors of the last century go unnoticed as the offspring of the baby boom generation continue to experience life in a virtual world. The inadequacy of a government school education is evident, when the MTV culture is stripped away and the core foundations of deficient understanding are exposed. The rapid spread of a global police state relies upon the suppression of truth and factual reality.

In this electronic age, when reading a book is considered a sentence of torture, the hash tag in a tweet is held out as grand sophistication. If surveyed, how many working age adults have ever read an Encyclopedia Britannica in a hardback edition? The point is that perception in images and sound bites is no substitute for thought, reflection and discernment.

The political messages and agenda for acceptable discourse are provided through filtered lenses presented as establishment news. The mainstream media, print, broadcast, televised, electronic and cultural all have in common a coordinated "Political Correctness" in content. The claims of diversity appear in every color, language and customs, while pushing the same reign of terror over the minds of critical thinking individuals.

The term alternative media is a pejorative slur to the power elites and screams out as an independent source of honest reporting to intrepid truth seekers. That often suspect source, Wikipedia, the free encyclopedia states: "Proponents of alternative media argue that the mainstream media often perpetuate traditional hegemonic power relations via their selection of content and their rhetorical and structural framing of news and information."

For economic insights, most subscribers to business news want predictions on stocks and portfolio performance. Placing emphasis on the political implications that affect business is often snubbed for latest trends in charts and money supply. This unfortunate disconnect that investment publications routinely ignore is seldom seen in the alternative business media. Primary importance of covering the forces and factions that stir political struggles is stressed in the economic reporting from non establishment media. There is no disconnection between money and politics. Independent news, investigative journalism and social commentary for it to be honest and reliable must be willing to confront and speak truth to power.

It is because this standard poses an existential and pragmatic threat to any established order, governments and institutions both fear and hate efforts to a wake public awareness and stamp out any sign of any populist outrage.

Since the internet has developed into a prime source of news for those who are electronically tuned in; the monopoly that the network TV, corporate radio news and conglomerate print gatekeepers once enjoyed has been breaking apart with a considerable loss of influence.

Before your elation that unorthodox and provocative reporting is becoming the new normal, the power elite strikes back. The virtual downright control over the legislative process, the Corporatist/State axis has the ability to pass laws that limit free speech. Add to this dilemma the power of the bureaucracy to regulate and executive orders to restrict effective political discourse and candid debate have a most formable obstacle to overcome.

Not all activists are endowed with unbridled courage. Computerworld reports that 75% of writers in free countries self-censor due to fears of mass surveillance.

THE PRESIDENT AND TWITTER

The US government has backed down under pressure from Twitter and the American Civil Liberties Union, withdrawing a request to unmask the identity of an account critical of President Donald Trump's immigration policy.

The withdrawal comes just one day after Twitter filed a lawsuit against the US Department of Homeland Security, secretary of homeland security John Kelly and the US Customs Border Protection, claiming users were protected under the first amendment.

In a new filing on Friday, Twitter said it was dismissing its previous complaint because the summons from the defendants had been withdrawn.

The lawsuit had threatened to spark the first legal clash between the new US administration and the technology industry. Many have been watching carefully to see if Mr Trump and traditionally Democratic Silicon Valley would conflict over issues such as free speech or encryption.

The defendants had asked the messaging platform to identify who was behind the Twitter account @ALT_USCIS, which is one of many protest accounts styling themselves as "alternative agencies" to comment on announcements made by government departments. It makes it clear it is not expressing the views of either the Department of Homeland Security or the customs agency.

Twitter argued that revealing the user's identity was necessary for the investigation of a criminal or civil offence. It said that users had the right to "anonymous and pseudonymous speech" to preserve their desire to speak freely and without fear of negative consequences from being the source of controversial views and commentary around the administration.

The ACLU had said it would represent the user behind the account and praised Twitter's decision to go to court to defend the user's right to anonymous speech.

Neither the Department for Homeland Security nor the customs agency responded to a request for comment. Twitter said it would not comment beyond the filing.

Shares in Twitter fell 0.6 percent to $14.31.

"US Drops Attempt to Unmask Anti-Trump Twitter Account," by Hannah Kuchler, The Financial Times Ltd, April 8, 2017.

The situation is getting worse, not better according to the recent PEN America report "Global Chilling: The Impact of Mass Surveillance on International Writers".

After 772 writers from 50 countries completed an online survey, PEN found that the results demonstrate "the damaging impact of surveillance by the United States and other governments on free expression and creative freedom around the world.

Now look at the account from ZDNet article, White House just endorsed CISPA measures, two years after veto threat.

"Given that the White House rightly criticized CISPA in 2013 for potentially facilitating the unnecessary transfer of personal information to the government or other private sector entities when sending cybersecurity threat data, we're concerned that the Administration proposal will unintentionally legitimize the approach taken by these dangerous bills," the Electronic Frontier Foundation said in a statement.

"CISPA 2015 would provide for an even cozier relationship between Silicon Valley and the US government at the detriment of civil liberties and privacy for everyone else," writer Rachael Tackett said on Tuesday.

A similarly-named bill Cybersecurity Information Sharing Act (CISA) made it through one of the Senate's committees, adding yet another legislative voice to the mix. Critics of the bill, however, called it an "even more toxic bill" than CISPA."

Both tech publications would not normally be considered part of the alternative media. Yet, from a perspective of imposing a climate of intimidation and implementing a data sucking collection system, the prospects of protecting a free exchange of ideas and news that is often critical of abusive authority is facing a real and present danger.

The future of an open and uncensored internet is very much in doubt. The reemergence of the printing press may well become the refuge of political incorrectness.

If the richest 1% may own half of global wealth by 2016, surely the even smaller 1% of that ominous 1% controls electoral politics, filters acceptable content in the mainstream media, enforces government decrees and maintains governance over society's institutions. The secular culture has no room for a counter voice of traditional values.

Allowing independent inquiry or social criticism to flourish online, risks the dominance of the establishment. However, the probability of public dissent to hit critical mass is far off. What now passes for critical thinking in universities is a shell of Aristotelian logic.

Since the average bottom feeder is so wrapped up in scrapping out a meager existence, most have no time or inclination to ponder the social and political issues of the day. This fact is well known by the elites who own, edit and present the daily chapter of contrived history that sadly passes as broadcast network news.

No matter what ideological bent one has, gathering your news from MSNBC, CNN or Fox News, just means your source of viewpoints cater to a political value that actually has no authentic values. Truth is seldom discovered within the mass media or from government propagandists.

US Media Executive Includes Russia Today (RT) in the same "Challenge List" as ISIS and Boko Haram, is an example of official state absurdity.

> Newly-appointed chief of US Broadcasting Board of Governors (BBG), Andrew Lack, has named RT one of the agency's main challenges alongside extremist groups like the Islamic State and Boko Haram.
>
> Lack, the first chief executive of the BBG, mentioned RT in an interview with The New York Times.
>
> "We are facing a number of challenges from entities like Russia Today which is out there pushing a point of view, the Islamic State in the Middle East and groups like Boko Haram," he said. "But I firmly believe that this agency has a role to play in facing those challenges."

This kind of assault on a foreign news network that frequently counters NATO strategy and the U.S. Empire is hard to believe that any stable person would accept such nonsense. So when the response in the account, Ex-BBG member: News outlets should never be compared to terrorists, it should be obvious that power politics surely outweighs open expression.

> "Comparing news outlets to terror organizations is jeopardizing the very foundations of freedom of speech in the US," Blanquita Cullum, ex-Broadcasting Board of Governors member, said after BBG's new boss placed RT on par with ISIS and Boko Haram.

RT is not part of the online alternative media *per se* but it certainly is outside the regurgitation of DC government press release reporting. Now if a major news network can be placed in the cross hairs for censoring, what chance do independent anti-establishment internet sites have to remain online long term?

Even when a sincere and concerned citizen wants to become educated and discovers a sage of wisdom and veracity that provides accurate information, most people prefer their dazed existence.

So the quandary is inescapable. The more successful alternative media becomes the more it will undergo the microscope of government tyrants. And achieving bigger victories for arousing the righteous anger of oppressed Americans, the more intense establishment attacks will become.

Will the *sheeple* grow up before the hammer hits the IP delete button?

> "At its core, hysteria substitutes for language when language becomes impossible: when words fail, or when I have no chance of making my meaning stick through reasoned argumentation, I, as hysteric, turn to the body and emotions as forms of articulation."

Alternative Media Has Taken Over "Fake News"

Maggie Hennefeld

In the following viewpoint, Maggie Hennefeld discusses the evolution of the term "fake news." Shows like The Daily Show, Last Week Tonight, *and* Full Frontal with Samantha Bee *used to fall under the umbrella of "fake news." But in the age of social media, another kind of "news" story has risen up to usurp that term. When genuinely falsified stories, such as the infamous "Pizzagate" conspiracy theory, gain traction in the communities of uneducated media consumers, they can be rebranded into blatant lies that are passed off as truth. The author claims that the future of debunking these falsehoods may fall on the shoulders of the satiric forms of truth-telling news. Hennefeld is a faculty member in the Cultural Studies and Comparative Literature department at the University of Minnesota.*

"Fake News: From Satirical Truthiness to Alternative Facts," by Maggie Hennefeld, New Politics, February 19, 2017. Reprinted by permission.

As you read, consider the following questions:

1. What are the major differences between "satirical news" and "fake news"?

2. Why is ambiguity important for those who perpetuate "fake news"?

3. How can satirical news shows combat those monopolizing on legitimate falsehoods?

In the wake of the 2016 election, Oxford Dictionaries declared "post-truth" to be the 2016 international word of the year. [i] The viral spread of fake news stories (such as the infamous "Pizzagate"[ii] scandal alleging that Hillary Clinton's campaign chair John Podesta secretly ran an illegal sex trafficking ring out of a Washington D.C. pizzeria) no doubt helped to install America's lunatic POTUS and his clown car of white supremacist cabinet members into the Oval Office.

In the halcyon days, the term "fake news" used to refer to hard-hitting satirical programs, in the vein of The Daily Show, The Colbert Report, Last Week Tonight, and Full Frontal with Samantha Bee. When the distinctions between truth and fiction, reality and absurdity, and authenticity and fakery have become so hopelessly blurred, comedic satire has felt like a last stand against the bottomless unreality of contemporary political media culture. Satire speaks truth to bull**** by usurping the very language of falsehood and nonsense.

In 2005, Stephen Colbert ironically declared "truthiness" to be "The Word" of the times.[iii] Re-watching this Colbert Report segment in 2017 feels like walking through a funhouse mirror. Truthiness, defined by Colbert as the fact that you don't "think with your head" but that you "know with your heart," has now become the lingua franca of Trumpist authoritarianism: it's a truth that comes from the gut (because "you have more nerve endings there"—just ask your gut). But displacing cold hard facts with heated emotions evidently has consequences.

Colbert quipped: "Who's Britannica to tell me that the Panama Canal was finished in 1914? If I want to say it was 1941, that's my right." Performing his parodic Fox News persona (modeled on Bill O'Reilly and Sean Hannity), Colbert proceeds to defend both the justness of the Iraq War and Bush's SCOTUS nomination of Harrier Miers as authentically truth-y, meanwhile skewering the dictionaries, encyclopedias, and reference books for being "all fact but no heart."

Recently, Trump's trusted counselor Kellyanne Conway has coined the term "alternative facts"[iv] (to rebrand abject lies), alleged a non-existent terrorist attack called "The Bowling Green Massacre"[v] (which the Internet promptly mocked as "too soon to laugh at" because we should wait until it actually happens), while Trump himself has taken to Twitter to perpetuate easily debunkable falsehoods on topics ranging from the weather and crowd size during his inauguration speech, to massive electoral voting fraud, to the unemployment and crime rates under Obama. Lies and fake news rule the day, while the Trump Administration's litany of absurdities blur with their comedic lampooning—nonstop ridiculous nonsense, but with catastrophic human and environmental consequences. It is perhaps fitting in this climate—when the distinction between fact and falsehood has been overtaken by the battle for earning more clicks and "likes" on social media—that satire, mockumentary hoax, and comedic buffoonery would represent among the last frontiers of political truth.

Beyond Colbert's prophetic vision of truthiness, the news satirist's slippery mode of truth-telling offers a powerful syntax for asserting just conviction against the relativism of objectivity and evidence. Laughter short-circuits the false opposition between the mind and the gut. It lends a critical comedic filter for managing the endemic desire to align truth not just with the evidence of objective reason, but with the satisfaction of emotional belief and moral conviction. In a political media climate driven by relentless spin, false equivalents, habitual instantaneity, hyper-mediation, and an overriding contradiction between the complexities of context and the need for easy sound bites, safeguarding the truth too often feels like an impossible leap of faith.

While "fake news" may always have been somewhat of a misnomer for comedic news satire, it is uncanny to see this once playful signifier so un-ironically repurposed in a political war of media disinformation. Sean Spicer (who reportedly chews and swallows two-and-a-half packs of Orbit cinnamon gum every day before noon[vi]), refused to answer questions from CNN or Buzzfeed, branding them "fake news!" at a White House Press Conference. Trump defended his unconstitutional immigration ban on Twitter, asserting that "any negative polls are fake news, just like the CNN, ABC, NBC polls in the election." Similarly, "the failing @nytimes does major FAKE NEWS China story."[vii] Fake news has become the catch-all signifier of an allegedly "post-truth" era, used to discredit or defame any truth that one simply does not like. Whoever has the strongest grip on power, or perhaps the loudest microphone, can thus dictate from whole cloth what's real and what's fake.

Yet, the fakery of fake news has always derived from its connotative ambiguity. This is the modus operandi of news satire from The Daily Show to The Yes Men to The Onion. For example, Andy Borowitz's satirical Borowitz Report recently noted: "Trump says he has been treated very unfairly by people who wrote Constitution."[viii] Though verifiably false, this certainly "feels true"—if not within the realm of something that Trump himself would plausibly Tweet. It is not hard to imagine Trump bemoaning the TOTAL DISTASTER of the U.S. Constitution and its crooked framers. An exercise in reductio ad absurdum— exposing illogic by taking problematic or dangerous rhetoric to its absurdist conclusions—satirical fake news dismantles bald-faced disinformation by debunking it not through science or reason but through the inherent absurdity of false logic.

On the eve of the inauguration, Michael Moore thus advised protesters to "fight Trump with an army of comedy."[ix] Given the extent to which comedic discourse and satire have effectively shaped the terms of Trump's candidacy and uniquely facilitated his political visibility, it seems inevitable that laughter would then hold the key to Trumpism's dismantling. Yet, satire always cuts both ways. Even a devastating joke can risk preempting action and dissent through the ideological echo chambers of reassuring laughter. Is there still room for play when the relativism of truth and politicization of language might help pave the way for the very censorship of the free press, the privatization of the social safety net, the erosion of environmental protections, and the escalation of a global arms race—if not worse?

As Masha Gessen has forebodingly described Trump's purchase on the truth, he "uses language to assert power over reality."[x] In a post-election interview with Samantha Bee on Full Frontal, Gessen further paraphrases Trump's unflagging bull****: "What he is saying is, 'I claim the right to say whatever the hell I please. And what are you gonna do about it?'" She compares Trump to the bully at the playground who steals your pencil box, hides it behind his back, and then claims not to have it in his hand. Against our protests, "But it's there, in your right hand!," the bully will insist, "But there's nothing in my right hand." In other words, "the point is not so much to take your pencil box, but to render you completely powerless, because everything you know how to do… is useless." "And you look foolish," Bee adds. "Yes," and, Gessen nails the coffin shut, "you don't get your box back either."

Gessen (an outspoken critic of Vladmir Putin, gay civil rights activist, and prolific public intellectual) had to flee from Putin's autocratic state—she is a political refugee, like many, with an ominous sense of déjà-vu. Her article, "Autocracy: Rules for Survival"[xi] (like Richard Rorty's Achieving Our Country[xii]), went viral after the election. In contrast to Rorty's tempered pragmatism, which extols the virtues of moral exceptionalism to combat the relativism of truth in postmodern culture, Gessen preaches the powers of mass hysteria. Her rules for survival include #1) Believe the autocrat; #2) Do not be taken in by small signs of normality; #3) Institutions will not save you; #4) Be outraged; #5)

Don't make compromises; and #6) Remember the future. Nicely condensing these six rules in her response to Bee's plea about what we can each do to resist, Gessen states bluntly: "The thing we can do…is actually to continue panicking. Continue to be the hysteric in the room"—[Bee interrupts, laughing, "I can stay hysterical!"]—Gessen: "Just continue panicking, write a note to yourself of what you would never do, and when you come to the line, don't cross it."

The language of authoritarianism is itself rather hysterical. When Trump addresses his supporters at a rally, his words appeal not to reason, or even to folksy common sense, but to emotional instinct. His chants of "Lock her up!," "Build a wall!," and "Make America Great Again!"—which range from illegal, to unactionable, to incomprehensible—solicit an overwhelming visceral response from the body of his exuberant supporter. It is precisely the jouissance of Trump's hysterical rally cries that make their targets (women, LGBTQ+, immigrants, people of color) feel so vulnerable and at risk in Trump's America. As many have commented, "take Trump seriously, not literally." If Trump "uses language to assert his power over reality," authenticating his meaning with hysterical emotion rather than intellectual persuasion, then responding with pervasive panic seems all too proportionate—especially given the autocratic lessons of twentieth-century history.

But what does it mean to "be the hysteric?" At its core, hysteria substitutes for language when language becomes impossible: when words fail, or when I have no chance of making my meaning stick through reasoned argumentation, I, as hysteric, turn to the body and emotions as forms of articulation. For example, nineteenth century female hysterics (who were represented as repressed middle-class women), suffered from fugue states, somnambulism, epileptic fits, and uncontrollable laughing, yawning, and hiccupping attacks in the absence of everyday words. Their theater of bodily symptoms substituted for their exclusion from the rational certitudes and enlightened positivism of masculinist public sphere discourse. Hysteria, not unlike comedic laughter, is an irrational means of expression that erupts from the very limits of conscious reason and symbolic language. (It is perhaps unsurprising that Freud, a preeminent theorist of female hysteria, also argued that women lack the mental apparatus for speaking truth to power as tendentious jokesters.)

In a recent piece on the underbelly of satire, "How Jokes Won the Election,"[xiii] New Yorker critic Emily Nussbaum associates the misogynistic, p****-grabbing, whitelash of Trumpism with "the explosion of female comedy" that "found its roots in everything from the female-cast Ghostbusters reboot to the anti-feminist GamerGate movement." She writes: "Trump's call to Make America Great Again was a plea to go back in time, to when people knew how to take a joke. It was an election about who owned the mike." Given the investment in excluding women from the powers of comedic invective, even the milder satire of a widely broadcast show like Saturday Night Live can play a politically consequential role in dismantling the oppressive ideologies of Trumpism.

As far as bullies go, Trump is notoriously thin-skinned—he's waged Twitter wars against comedians including Alec Baldwin, Jon Stewart, Bill Maher, Rosie O'Donnell, and pretty much the entire cast of SNL. It is undeniably fun to get Trump's goat. For example, Melissa McCarthy's outrageous burlesque of Sean Spicer has already spurred an energetic movement for women to play each member of Trump's Administration (such as O'Donnell as Steve Bannon, Ellen DeGeneres as Mike Pence, Betty White as Jeff Sessions, and Meryl Streep as Donald Trump).[xiv] Even the laughter of ad hominem satire is still pointed enough to prick the fragile ego of Trumpist authoritarianism.

While the political law-makers are seizing their monopoly on legitimate falsehoods, the satirists must consolidate their purchase on truthiness. Alongside the facts, absurdist invective has the traction to dislodge falsehoods that are somehow too verifiably inaccurate to debunk through objective or referential means. If fact checking "alt-facts" often feels more absurd than consequential, then why not fight the cynicism of false consciousness with the absurdism of disbelief? It will be a war of consensus between the propaganda of fake-fake news (as disinformation) and the critical apparatus of real-fake news (as comedic truth-telling).

In early February, at a breakfast meeting to kick off Black History Month, Trump made comments praising the 19th century Black abolitionist Frederick Douglass, indicating that he has no idea who Douglass actually is and that he still believes Douglass to be alive. Trump proclaimed: he is "an example of somebody who's done an amazing job and is being recognized more and more, I've noticed." Shortly afterward, the fake Twitter account @realFrederickDouglass was also declaring "MASSIVE VOTER FRAUD that led to black ppl and women not voting for entire first half of U.S. history!"[xv] In related news, @realFrederickDouglass recently checked in on Facebook and was marked safe at #BowlingGreenMassacre. When the line between #real and verifiably fake has become dangerously obscure, we must also look to satire to show us the truth.

Notes

[i] https://www.oxforddictionaries.com/press/news/2016/12/11/WOTY-16

[ii] https://en.wikipedia.org/wiki/Pizzagate_conspiracy_theory

[iii] http://www.cc.com/video-clips/63ite2/the-colbert-report-the-word---truthiness

[iv] https://www.washingtonpost.com/news/the-fix/wp/2017/01/22/how-kellyanne-conway-ushered-in-the-era-of-alternative-facts/?utm_term=.f037ef4ea981

[v] https://en.wikipedia.org/wiki/Bowling_Green_massacre

[vi] http://nymag.com/thecut/2017/01/sean-spicer-swallows-35-pieces-of-gum-every-day-before-noon.html

[vii] https://twitter.com/realDonaldTrump/status/830047626414477312

[viii] http://www.newyorker.com/humor/borowitz-report/trump-says-he-has-been-treated-very-unfairly-by-people-who-wrote-constitution

[ix] https://grassrootscomedy.com/2017/01/27/michael-moore-fight-donald-trump-with-an-army-of-comedy/

[x] https://www.youtube.com/watch?v=rwQeKSlY56Q

[xi] http://www.nybooks.com/daily/2016/11/10/trump-election-autocracy-rules-for-survival/

[xii] http://www.hup.harvard.edu/catalog.php?isbn=9780674003125

[xiii] http://www.newyorker.com/magazine/2017/01/23/how-jokes-won-the-election

[xiv] http://www.huffingtonpost.com/zac-thompson/snl-should-cast-only-wome_b_14642374.html

[xv] http://onehotmessalaska.blogspot.com/2017/02/frederick-douglass-opens-twitter.html

| "The rise in satire is a sign of the
health of our democracy."

Satire Has Risen Up to Become a Legitimate News Source

Sophia A. McClennen

In the following viewpoint, Sophia A. McClennen argues that satirical news has taken a major role in shaping voter perceptions. With the growing popularity of news-centric comedy offerings like The Daily Show, Saturday Night Live, *and* The Onion, *it is impossible to keep satire out of elections. Satirical news helps inform the electorate and creates legitimate competition to the traditional sources of news, to the point where people who do shape their political perceptions from these traditional broadcast entities are considered underinformed in comparison. McClennen is professor of International Affairs and Comparative Literature at Penn State University.*

As you read, consider the following questions:

1. What percentage of Americans under the age of 40 say that satirical news is overtaking traditional news?
2. How is the 24/7 news cycle in traditional news doing damage to its attempts to inform the electorate?
3. Is satire good for American democracy, in the author's opinion?

"Does Satire News Influence Elections?" by Sophia A. McClennen, December 31, 2014. Reprinted by permission.

As Election Day looms, *The Daily Show* ramped up their media coverage by heading to Texas for a week of shows entitled *Democalypse 2014: South by South Mess*. A Comedy Central show relocated to broadcast on-the-spot election coverage. That should strike us as strange, right? But in all likelihood, it doesn't. The idea that a satire news show would take election coverage so seriously no longer comes as a surprise. How did satire news become such a major player in news media? And, is its increased social power dangerous for our democracy?

Let's start with the facts. Satire news today plays a major role in shaping voter perceptions. If you think back on recent election coverage, chances are that at least some of your memories of "news" coverage include satire. Maybe you recall *The Daily Show*'s coverage of the Florida governor's race, John Oliver's mockery of the GOP efforts to rebrand, or Stephen Colbert's Twitter-mocking of Louisiana Governor Bobby Jindal. Maybe you read *The Onion*'s piece "Midterm Candidates Distancing Selves from United States."

But beyond the anecdotal we now know that satire news is increasingly overtaking mainstream news as a source of voter information, especially for younger and left-leaning voters. A 2009 Rasmussen poll showed that nearly one-third of Americans under the age of 40 say satirical news-oriented television programs like *The Colbert Report* and *The Daily Show* are taking the place of traditional news outlets. Further research by the Pew Research Center from 2012 showed that among younger millennial-aged voters satire news was not only more common, but also more trusted.

This trend has been surging over the last few elections. It's worth recalling that *The Daily Show* has gone on the road every two years either for coverage live from the Democrat and Republican conventions, or in midterm years, to locations they considered central to major races. They traveled to D.C. in 2002 and 2010, and visited the swing state of Ohio in 2006. On October 30, 2008 Stewart and Colbert held a pre-midterm rally on the National

Mall that attracted a live audience of over 200,000 and 2.5 million live viewers.

There have been some extremely noteworthy satire moments in the last few elections: Who could forget the role that Colbert played in educating viewers on campaign finance by starting his own Super PAC and then encouraging his viewers to do the same? And then there was Tina Fey's impersonation of Sarah Palin that played a key role in drawing voters away from the McCain-Palin ticket. And it goes beyond the professional satirists too: average citizens are tweeting, facebooking, snapchatting, and creating satirical memes that often go viral. Entire twitter accounts, for instance, are satirical. The satirical Twitter feed for "Top Conservative Cat," who describes as a "Colbert conservative," has over 104,000 followers on Twitter.

This is all goes to show that satire is everywhere and that it's increasingly a part of the media diet of younger, more left-leaning voters. But this trend can't be good for our democracy, right? Satire is a form of mockery; it can't possibly teach voters how to respect the values at the core of our nation. If anything, the rise in satire is a sign of the demise of our nation. Or is it?

Actually, the rise in satire is a sign of the health of our democracy. And we have a range of data to prove it. First of all, a study conducted by the Pew Research Center has shown that viewers of programs like *The Daily Show* and *The Colbert Report* actually score higher for accuracy on current events than viewers of programs like *The O'Reilly Factor* or *The NewsHour with Jim Lehrer*. They also score higher than viewers of cable news sources like CNN and Fox News. This research is backed by a number of other studies, including one by the Annenburg Public Policy Center that proved that Colbert's Super PAC stunt worked as a civics lesson.

Satire news has stepped up to help inform the electorate at a complex moment in news media history. The 24/7 television news cycle is now almost totally dominated by opinion, expert debates, punditry, and other forms of fluff that don't actually offer viewers much in terms of objective information. The result is that viewers that watch Fox News, for instance, are less informed about political information than viewers that watch no news at all. And, to make it worse, they are more likely to believe misinformation.

Young news consumers, in contrast, are more apt to question the source of their information and satire news viewers are more likely to trust Jon Stewart than Fox News, CNN, or MSNBC as a source of news. And this from voters that are reaching new lows in levels of trust in politicians, the media, and other authority figures. Too often television news today media packages information in stark oppositions that then allow "experts" to present opposite points of view. Often the oppositions are based on false binaries, faulty logic, or sheer hyperbole. Such a format does not enhance the critical thinking necessary for informed democratic participation.

Many often falsely blame the satirists for the state of news, when it is satire that simply comments on and calls attention to the flaws in our media and politicians. Satire trades in exposing falsehoods, mocking poor thinking, and laughing at folly. Satire works by asking the audience to think critically and to question the status quo. In this way, satirists like Stewart, Colbert, and Oliver function as a corrective for the sensational, often silly, news that is reported on cable television. If there were no flaws in the system, there would be nothing for them to mock.

And this is why the increased role of satire news in our democracy is a positive sign. For the first time in U.S. history a range of satirical news sources are providing the public with valuable information from which to make educated decisions. Our knowledge as voters may be coming from HBO and Comedy Central instead of Fox News, MSNBC, and CNN, but the satire news is helping us stay informed and stay productively critical. Contrary to some criticism, satire's goal is not voter apathy; its goal is to encourage voters to turn their disgust into action and their frustrations into votes.

Periodical and Internet Sources Bibliography

The following articles have been selected to supplement the diverse views presented in this chapter.

Senator Richard Burr (R-NC), "S.754—To improve cybersecurity in the United States through enhanced sharing of information about cybersecurity threats, and for other purposes." Congress.gov, March 17, 2015. https://www.congress.gov/bill/114th-congress/senate-bill/754.

Anthony Leiserowitz, Edward Maibach, Connie Roser-Renouf, Seth Rosenthal, AND Matthew Cutler, "Climate Change in the American Mind: May 2017," Yale Program on Climate Change Communication, July 5, 2017. http://climatecommunication.yale.edu/publications/climate-change-american-mind-may-2017/.

Greg Lukianoff and Jonathan Hadit, "The Coddling of the American Mind," *Atlantic*, September 2015. https://www.theatlantic.com/magazine/archive/2015/09/the-coddling-of-the-american-mind/399356/.

PEN's International Survey of Writers, "Global Chilling: The Impact of Mass Surveillance on International Writers," PEN America, January 5, 2014. https://pen.org/global-chilling-the-impact-of-mass-surveillance-on-international-writers/.

Samantha Schmidt and Lindsey Bever, "Kellyanne Conway Cites 'Bowling Green Massacre' That Never Happened to Defend Travel Ban," *Washington Post*, February 3, 2017. https://www.washingtonpost.com/news/morning-mix/wp/2017/02/03/kellyanne-conway-cites-bowling-green-massacre-that-never-happened-to-defend-travel-ban/?utm_term=.cd66d4c62552.

Rebecca Sinderbrand, "How Kellyanne Conway Ushered in the Era of 'Alternative facts,'" *Washington Post*, January 22, 2017. https://www.washingtonpost.com/news/the-fix/wp/2017/01/22/how-kellyanne-conway-ushered-in-the-era-of-alternative-facts/?utm_term=.e54ba056c514.

For Further Discussion

Chapter 1

1. With so many people getting their news from social media, how is it possible to have an educated society when a person can become trapped in an online filter bubble? Explain your answer with examples from the chapter's viewpoints.
2. Do companies such as Google, Apple, and Microsoft have an obligation to shut down websites that are potentially malicious because they aim to misinform their readers and potentially infect their consumers' computers with malware? Why or why not?
3. Mary Louise Kelly discusses the CIA's conclusion that Russia interfered with the 2016 United States presidential election. Should the government have done more to inform the public of this interference while Barack Obama was still president?

Chapter 2

1. Use Ben Debney's discussion of the differences between "radicalization" and "extremism" to discuss how Western governments can do better when attempting to spread democracy in the Middle East.
2. Consider the way the media covers violent extremism to discuss the importance of educating the public. Is it possible to have fair and open coverage and education of extremist action in other countries? Why or why not?
3. Discuss the importance of having a country's political electorate educated on such matters from a young age. How can younger voters find accurate political coverage when they may come from ideologically skewed families or backgrounds? Find three primary examples and elaborate on them.

Chapter 3

1   Discuss the future of free and open discourse on the Internet, along with three potential roadblocks toward that future. How can we overcome these roadblocks?

2. In the United States, freedom of the press is protected by the First Amendment. Why is it important to ensure continued freedom of the press in the United States, with passing of acts like the Daniel Pearl Freedom of the Press Act. How does press freedom in democratic countries foster press freedom in nondemocratic countries?

3. With the growth of the Internet comes the growth of actions like cyber terrorism. Eliminating safe havens for cyber terrorists in certain countries is one of the first steps toward stopping these actions. Using Fawzia Casim's viewpoint, discuss what steps should be taken next to stop cyber terrorism in digital society.

Chapter 4

1. With the advent of the Internet and new forms of media, discuss the future of traditional and mainstream media. How can they catch up? Will they catch up? Using examples from Denise Robbins's viewpoint on climate change, what is another example of a topic that is not covered well by the mainstream media?

2. Identify some of the negative aspects and tendencies of the mainstream media. How does alternative media have the potential to combat these problems?

3. Using the views expressed in both Maggie Hennefeld and Sophia A. McClennen's viewpoints, discuss the growing place for satire in political discourse. How can "hard news" media outlets "catch up" so that they can better inform their consumers? If you disagree, why is there a place for ideologically skewed media outlets in today's society?

Organizations to Contact

The editors have compiled the following list of organizations concerned with the issues debated in this book. The descriptions are derived from materials provided by the organizations. All have publications or information available for interested readers. The list was compiled on the date of publication of the present volume; the information provided here may change. Be aware that many organizations take several weeks or longer to respond to inquiries, so allow as much time as possible.

AlterNet

77 Federal Street, Second Floor, San Francisco, CA 94107
(415) 284-1420
website: www.alternet.org

AlterNet is an award-winning news magazine and online community whose aim is to inspire action and advocacy on the environment, human rights and civil liberties, social justice, media, health care issues, and more.

American Civil Liberties Union

125 Broad Street, 18th Floor, New York, NY 10004
(212) 549-2500
website: www.aclu.org

For almost 100 years, the ACLU has worked to defend and preserve the individual rights and liberties guaranteed by the Constitution and laws of the United States.

Anti-Defamation League

(202) 452-8310
email: adlmedia@adl.org
website: www.adl.org

The ADL is dedicated to stopping anti-Semitism and defending the Jewish people and fights threats to democracy, including cyberhate, bullying, bias in schools and the criminal justice system, terrorism, hate crimes, coercion of religious minorities, and contempt for anyone who is different.

Cato Institute

1000 Massachusetts Avenue NW, Washington, DC 20001
(202) 842-0200
email: cato@cato.org
website: www.cato.org

The Cato Institute is a public policy research organization dedicated to the principles of individual liberty, limited government, free markets, and peace. Its scholars and analysts conduct independent, nonpartisan research on a wide range of policy issues.

Center for American Progress

1333 H Street NW, 10ᵗʰ Floor, Washington, DC 20005
(202) 682-1611
website: www.americanprogress.org

The Center for American Progress is an independent nonpartisan policy institute that is dedicated to improving the lives of all Americans, through bold, progressive ideas, as well as strong leadership and concerted action.

Center for Constitutional Rights

666 Broadway 7ᵗʰ Floor, New York, NY 10012
(212) 614-6473
email: press@ccrjustice.org
website: ccrjustice.org

The Center for Constitutional Rights is dedicated to advancing and protecting the rights guaranteed by the United States Constitution and the Universal Declaration of Human Rights. CCR is committed to the creative use of law as a positive force for social change.

First Amendment Coalition

534 Fourth Street, Suite B, San Rafael, CA 94901
(415) 460-5060
email: fac@firstamendmentcoalition.org
website: firstamendmentcoalition.org

The mission of the First Amendment Coalition is to protect and promote freedom of expression and the people's right to know. The coalition is a nonprofit, nonpartisan educational and advocacy organization serving the public, public servants, and the media in all its forms.

The International Consortium of Investigative Journalists

910 17th Street NW, Suite 410, Washington, DC 20006
website: www.icij.org

The International Consortium of Investigative Journalists is a global network of more than 190 investigative journalists in more than 65 countries who collaborate on in-depth investigative stories focusing on issues that do not stop at national frontiers: cross-border crime, corruption, and the accountability of power.

The Nieman Foundation for Journalism at Harvard University

One Francis Avenue, Cambridge, MA 02138
(617) 495-2237
email: staff@niemanlab.org
website: www.niemanlab.org

The Nieman Journalism Lab is an attempt to help journalism figure out its future in an Internet age. It wants to help reporters and editors adjust to their online labors; it wants to help traditional news organizations find a way to survive; it wants to help the new crop of startups that will complement—or supplant—them.

Online News Association

1111 North Capitol Street NE, 6th Floor, Washington, DC 20002
(202) 503-9222
email: irving@journalists.org
website: www.journalists.org

The Online News Association is the world's largest association of digital journalists. ONA's mission is to inspire innovation and excellence among journalists to better serve the public.

ProPublica

155 Avenue of the Americas, 13th Floor, New York, NY 10013
(212) 514-5250
email: info@propublica.org
website: www.propublica.org

ProPublica is an independent, nonprofit newsroom that produces investigative journalism in the public interest. It produces journalism that shines a light on exploitation of the weak by the strong and on the failures of those with power to vindicate the trust placed in them.

Society of Professional Journalists

3909 N. Meridian Street, Indianapolis, IN 46208
(317)-927-8000
email: agutierrez@spj.org
website: www.spj.org

The Society of Professional Journalists is the nation's most broad-based journalism organization, dedicated to encouraging the free practice of journalism and stimulating high standards of ethical behavior.

Bibliography of Books

Finn Brunton, *Spam: A Shadow History of the Internet.* Cambridge, MA: MIT Press, 2013.

W. Joseph Campbell, *Getting It Wrong: Debunking the Greatest Myths in American Journalism.* Berkeley, CA: University of California Press, 2016.

Eric Deggans, *Race-Baiter: How the Media Wields Dangerous Words to Divide a Nation.* New York, NY: St. Martin's Press, 2012.

Matthew Fuller and Andrew Goffey, *Evil Media.* Cambridge, MA: MIT Press, 2012.

Howard Gardner and Katie Davis, *The App Generation: How Today's Youth Navigate Identity, Intimacy, and Imagination in a Digital World.* New Haven, CT: Yale University Press, 2013.

Juan Gonzalez and Joseph Torres, *News for All The People: The Epic Story of Race and the American Media.* London: Verso, 2012.

Virginia Heffernan, *Magic and Loss: The Internet as Art.* New York, NY: Simon & Schuster, 2016.

Ryan Holiday, *Trust Me, I'm Lying: Confessions of a Media Manipulator.* London: Portfolio, 2012.

Henry Jenkins, Sam Ford, and Joshua Green, *Spreadable Media: Creating Value and Meaning in a Networked Culture (Postmillennial Pop).* New York, NY: NYU Press, 2012.

Elliot King, *Free for All: The Internet's Transformation of Journalism.* Evanston, IL: Northwestern University Press, 2010.

Jaron Lanier, *Who Owns the Future?* New York, NY: Simon & Schuster, 2013.

Alice E.Marwick, *Status Update: Celebrity, Publicity, and Branding in the Social Media Age.* New Haven, CT: Yale University Press, 2013.

Kelly McBride and Tom Rosensteil, *The New Ethics of Journalism: Principles for the 21st Century.* Washington, DC: CQ Press, 2013.

Nicco Mele, *The End of Big: How the Internet Makes David the New Goliath.* New York, NY: St. Martin's Press, 2013.

Eric Schmidt and Jared Cohen, *The New Digital Age: Reshaping the Future of People, Nations and Business.* London: Hodder & Stoughton, 2013.

Joel Simon, *The New Censorship: Inside the Global Battle for Media Freedom.* New York, NY: Columbia University Press, 2014.

Mitchell Stephens, *Beyond News: The Future of Journalism.* New York, NY: Columbia University Press, 2014.

Index

satirical news, 146–147, 178, 179–184, 186–189

self-censuring, 171–177

Shaaban, Bouthania, 64–81

Slate, 151

Sleeper, Jim, 154–170

Snowden, Edward, 21

social media, growth of, 88

Syria, 64–81

T

technology and alternative media, 88–143

terrorism, 51, 53, 54, 56–57, 59, 60, 61, 65, 67, 70, 72, 74, 78–79, 80, 177

  cyber terrorism, 107–117

Trump, Donald, 17, 27, 28–30, 83, 174, 179, 180, 181–185

Turkey, 58, 59, 61, 62, 63, 67, 68, 69, 71, 74, 77, 80

Twitter, 36, 146, 171, 172, 174, 180, 184, 188

U

Unmüßig, Barbara, 90–96

Upworthy, 149–150

W

WikiLeaks, 15, 18, 28, 31, 33–41, 46

Y

yellow journalism, 75

Z

Zheng, Haiping, 130–143

Zuckerburg, Mark, 17